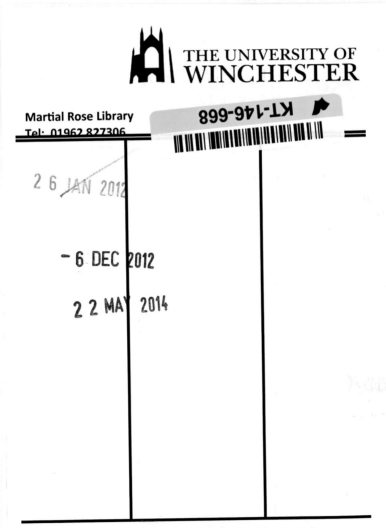

Catherine Belsey is Professor of English at Cardiff University, where she chairs the Centre for Critical and Cultural Theory. Her books include *Desire: Love Stories in Western Culture* and *Shakespeare and the Loss of Eden*

IN THE SAME SERIES

Catherine
Belsey

Critical Practice

2nd Edition

Routledge
Taylor & Francis Group

LONDON AND NEW YORK

First published in 1980 by Methuen & Co. Ltd
Reprinted six times

Reprinted 1988, 1989, 1990, 1991, 1992, 1993,
1994, 1996, 1999, 2001
by Routledge
11 New Fetter Lane, London EC4P 4EE

Simultaneously published in the USA and Canada
by Routledge
29 West 35th Street, New York, NY 10001

This edition first published 2002 by Routledge

Routledge is an imprint of the Taylor & Francis Group

© 1980, 2002 Catherine Belsey

Typeset in Joanna by RefineCatch Limited, Bungay, Suffolk
Printed and bound in Great Britain by
TJ International Ltd, Padstow, Cornwall

British Library Cataloguing in Publication Data
A catalogue record for this book is available from the British Library

Library of Congress Cataloging in Publication Data
A catalog record for this book has been requested

ISBN 0–415–28005–2 (Hbk)
ISBN 0–415–28006–0 (Pbk)

CONTENTS

GENERAL EDITOR'S PREFACE

No doubt a third General Editor's Preface to *New Accents* seems hard to justify. What is there left to say? Twenty-five years ago, the series began with a very clear purpose. Its major concern was the newly perplexed world of academic literary studies, where hectic monsters called 'Theory', 'Linguistics' and 'Politics' ranged. In particular, it aimed itself at those undergraduates or beginning postgraduate students who were either learning to come to terms with the new developments or were being sternly warned against them.

New Accents deliberately took sides. Thus the first Preface spoke darkly, in 1977, of 'a time of rapid and radical social change', of the 'erosion of the assumptions and presuppositions' central to the study of literature. 'Modes and categories inherited from the past' it announced, 'no longer seem to fit the reality experienced by a new generation'. The aim of each volume would be to 'encourage rather than resist the process of change' by combining nuts-and-bolts exposition of new ideas with clear and detailed explanation of related conceptual developments. If mystification (or downright demonisation) was the enemy, lucidity (with a nod to the compromises inevitably at stake there) became a friend. If a 'distinctive discourse of the future' beckoned, we wanted at least to be able to understand it.

With the apocalypse duly noted, the second Preface proceeded piously to fret over the nature of whatever rough beast might stagger portentously from the rubble. 'How can we recognise or deal with the new?', it complained, reporting nevertheless the dismaying advance of 'a host of barely respectable activities for which we have no reassuring names' and promising a programme of wary surveillance at 'the boundaries of the precedented and at the limit of the thinkable'. Its conclusion, 'the unthinkable, after all, is that which covertly shapes our thoughts' may rank as a truism. But in so far as it offered some sort of useable purchase on a world of crumbling certainties, it is not to be blushed for.

In the circumstances, any subsequent, and surely final, effort can only modestly look back, marvelling that the series is still here, and not unreasonably congratulating itself on having provided an initial outlet for what turned, over the years, into some of the distinctive voices and topics in literary studies. But the volumes now re-presented have more than a mere historical interest. As their authors indicate, the issues they raised are still potent, the arguments with which they engaged are still disturbing. In short, we weren't wrong. Academic study did change rapidly and radically to match, even to help to generate, wide-reaching social changes. A new set of discourses was developed to negotiate those upheavals. Nor has the process ceased. In our deliquescent world, what was unthinkable inside and outside the academy all those years ago now seems regularly to come to pass.

Whether the *New Accents* volumes provided adequate warning of, maps for, guides to, or nudges in the direction of this new terrain is scarcely for me to say. Perhaps our best achievement lay in cultivating the sense that it was there. The only justification for a reluctant third attempt at a Preface is the belief that it still is.

TERENCE HAWKES

ACKNOWLEDGEMENTS

I should like to acknowledge the very considerable help I have received from Margaret Atack, Michael Comber, Peter Foulkes, John Hartley, Philip Simpson and Alan Waite. I am grateful too to the General Editor, Terence Hawkes, who has been consistently encouraging but firm; to Christopher Norris and Chris Weedon for a number of valuable comments on the manuscript; to the Joneses, whose neighbourly windows have been a constant resource; and to Andrew Belsey, whose constructive scepticism kept me going.

PREFACE TO THE SECOND EDITION

Writing the first edition of *Critical Practice* was a learning experience for me. New theories were arriving from Paris by the planeload, giving rise to heated debate. They seemed to change everything we thought about culture in general, but there was only one way to find out what difference they made to the practice of reading in particular. How do we know what we think till we see what we write? I wrote the book to find out – and have never been the same since.

At that time the principal influences were Roland Barthes, whose scintillating *S/Z* represented my first encounter with post-Saussurean criticism, and Louis Althusser, who made clear that the educational institution was a place where cultural values were both inculcated and contested. Jacques Lacan was there, at least in the first instance, as an influence on Althusser. Michel Foucault was beginning to be there too, but not pre-eminently as a commentator on fiction or the literary institution. We did not yet know that his term, 'discourse', would come in English to mean everything cultural, and nothing in particular. Jacques Derrida had not at that time made much impact in the UK: I was under the impression that, in contrast to the Marxism of Althusser and Pierre Macherey, Derridean deconstruction was predominantly formalist. I could hardly have been more wrong: the logic of deconstruction has the effect of dismantling the founding assumptions of Western philosophy in its entirety.

Times have changed, and *Critical Practice* needs updating to take account of what we know now. Knowledge is like that: our current understanding will, no doubt, be superseded in its turn. To keep that temporal relativity in view, I have not tried to eliminate all elements of the period flavour of the first edition. But I have erased what would now mislead readers, and I have added a chapter on the critical implications of deconstruction, without seeing any reason to set it against the politics of Althusser and Macherey. Hasn't Derrida himself acknowledged the contribution of revolutionary political analysis in *Specters of Marx*?

One of the changes since I wrote the book has been an expansion of critical positions: feminism was well established at that time, but not queer studies or postcolonialism. As far as I am concerned, the new developments are extremely welcome: the more radical readings there are, the better. But committed as I am to the success of queer and postcolonial politics, I have not isolated them in the second edition as distinct practices, any more than I isolated feminism in the first, though it was repeatedly present in the examples I gave. With the best of intentions, the understanding of critical theory as a succession of 'isms', the text read now from one political position, now from another, has done, in my view, more harm than good, giving the impression that reading is a matter of personal values.

The concern of *Critical Practice* is not our individual commitments, not what we read, nor what politics we bring to bear on what we read (though my own sympathies are transparently clear in the text), but the reading process itself. Methodologically, it is perfectly possible for a Marxist to read no differently from a conservative, or for a feminist to limit the possibilities of intrepretation to making character-sketches. Politics alone changes nothing much. My interest is in the transformation brought about in our sense of what a text is, as well as what reading is, by the theories developed in France after the Second World War on the basis of the linguistics of Ferdinand de Saussure. The critical practice that becomes available in consequence has radical possibilities for a range of political positions.

Chapter 1 is beginning to seem from my point of view a matter primarily of historical interest. I have let it stand, however: expressive realism, the traditional way of understanding the text as a means of access to the author's view of life, is still to be found in unexpected places, not least the book reviews in the Sunday papers and the cultural programmes on television, and it may well be the starting-point of students new to theory. The succession of assaults on it I chart, some more successful than others, are evidence that there was a strong sense in the critical institution of its inadequacy, even before post-Saussurean theory gave us a clear alternative. But the new theories are now much more widespread, much more respectable, than they were, and I have therefore isolated these earlier challenges in a second chapter, which readers who feel justified in ignoring the history of criticism are welcome to skip.

I have added a completely new set of suggestions for further reading, since nothing dates faster than bibliographies. But the classic texts have aged well. They were in many ways ahead of their time.

So, in my view, was the New Accents series as a whole, which took on a declining critical and cultural tradition and made a difference. It is a privilege to have been involved.

Catherine Belsey
January 2002

1

TRADITIONAL CRITICISM AND COMMON SENSE

COMMONSENSE CRITICISM

In David Lodge's novel, *Changing Places*, Philip Swallow finds, when he arrives as Visiting Professor of English at an American university, that he has been put down to teach a course on novel-writing. A student called Wily Smith is eager to take the course.

> 'I have this novel I want to write. It's about this black kid growing up in the ghetto. . . .'
>
> 'Isn't that going to be rather difficult?' said Philip. 'I mean, unless you actually *are*. . . .'
>
> Philip hesitated. He had been instructed by Charles Boon that 'black' was the correct usage these days, but he found himself unable to pronounce a word associated in Rummidge with the crudest kind of racial prejudice. 'Unless you've had the experience yourself', he amended his sentence.
>
> 'Sure. Like the story is autobiographical. All I need is technique.'
>
> 'Autobiographical?' Philip scrutinized the young man, narrowing his eyes and cocking his head to one side. Wily Smith's complexion was about the shade of Philip's own a week after his summer

holiday, when his tan would begin to fade and turn yellow. 'Are you
sure?'

'Sure I'm sure.' Wily Smith looked hurt, not to say insulted.

(Lodge 1978: 67)

Whatever difficulties of intercultural communication are involved,
professor and student share an assumption that novels are about life,
that they are written from personal experience and that this is the
source of their authenticity. They share, in other words, the commonsense view of literature, which proposes a practice of reading in
quest of expressive realism, and the only alternative offered in *Changing
Places* is the literary imperialism of the encyclopaedic Morris Zapp,
entrepreneurial descendant of Northrop Frye. Common sense assumes
that valuable literary texts, those which are in a special way worth
reading, tell truths – about the period that produced them, about the
world in general, or about human nature – and that in doing so, they
express the particular perceptions, the individual insights, of their
authors.

Common sense also offers this way of approaching literature not as a
self-conscious and deliberate practice, a method based on a reasoned
theoretical position, but as the 'obvious' mode of reading, the 'natural'
way of approaching literary works. Critical theory accordingly appears
as a perfectly respectable but to some degree peripheral area, almost a
distinct discipline, a suitable activity for graduate students, or perhaps
to be got out of the way as an introductory 'isms course' for undergraduates, while having no necessary connection with the practice of
reading itself. To a few diehards, it seems misleading, interfering with
the natural way of reading, perplexing the minds of readers with nice
speculations of philosophy, and so leading to over-ingenuity, jargon
and a loss of direct and spontaneous contact with the immediately
perceptible reality of the text.

THE NEW THEORIES

Meanwhile, recent work in Europe and in the United States, stimulated
above all from France, has called in question not only some of the
specific assumptions of common sense, some of the beliefs which

appear most obvious and natural, but the authority of common sense itself, the collective and timeless wisdom whose unquestioned presence seems to be the source and guarantee of everything we take for granted. This work may be labelled 'poststructuralist', but I have identified it here as 'post-Saussurean', to emphasize its line of descent from the radical elements in the linguistic theory of Ferdinand de Saussure. Post-Saussurean theory proposes that common sense itself is ideologically and discursively constructed, rooted in a specific historical situation, and operating in conjunction with a particular social formation. In other words, it is argued that what seems obvious and natural is not necessarily so but that, on the contrary, the 'obvious' and the 'natural' are not *given* but produced in a specific society by the ways in which that society talks and thinks about itself and its experience.

It follows that the propositions of common sense concerning the practice of reading are also in question. Post-Saussurean work on language has challenged the whole concept of realism; Roland Barthes has specifically proclaimed the death of the author; and Jacques Lacan, Louis Althusser and Jacques Derrida have all from various positions questioned the humanist assumption that the individual mind or inner being is the source of meaning and truth. In this context, the notion of a text which tells a (or the) truth, as perceived by an individual subject (the author), whose insights are the source of the text's single and authoritative meaning, is not only untenable, but literally unthinkable, because the problematic which supported it, the framework of assumptions and knowledges, ways of thinking, probing and analysing that it was based on, no longer stands.

In practice, common sense betrays its own inadequacy by its incoherences, its contradictions and its silences. Presenting itself as non-theoretical, as 'obvious', common sense is not called on to demonstrate that it is internally consistent. But an account of the world which finally proves to be incoherent or non-explanatory constitutes an unsatisfactory foundation for the practice either of reading or of criticism. Empiricist common sense, however, effaces this problem by urging that the real task of the critic is to get on with the reading process, to respond directly to the text without worrying about niceties of theory, as if the lack of any systematic approach or procedure were a guarantee of objectivity. In this way, empiricism evades confrontation with its own propositions, protects whatever values and methods are currently dominant, and so guarantees the very opposite of objectivity, the perpetuation of unquestioned assumptions.

But there is no practice without theory, however much that theory is suppressed, unformulated or perceived as 'obvious'. What we do when we read, however natural it seems, presupposes a whole theoretical vocabulary, even if unspoken, which defines certain relationships between meaning and the world, meaning and people, and finally people themselves and their place in the world.

Common sense appears obvious because it is inscribed in the language we speak. Post-Saussurean theory, therefore, starts from an analysis of language, proposing that language is not transparent, not merely the *medium* in which autonomous individuals transmit messages to each other about an independently constituted world of things. On the contrary, it is language which offers the possibility of constructing a world of distinct individuals and things, and of differentiating between them. The transparency of language is an illusion.

OPACITY

Partly as a consequence of this theory, the language used by its practitioners is usually far from transparent. The effect of this is to alert the reader to the opacity of language, and to avoid the 'tyranny of lucidity', the impression that what is being said must be true simply because it is clear and familiar. The modes of address of post-Saussurean writers like Louis Althusser, Roland Barthes, Jacques Derrida and Jacques Lacan, though different from each other in important ways, share this property of difficulty, and not simply from a perverse desire to be obscure. To challenge familiar assumptions and familiar values in a vocabulary which, in order to be easily readable, is compelled to reproduce these assumptions and values, is an impossibility. New concepts, new theories, necessitate new, unfamiliar and therefore initially difficult terms.

For instance, I shall introduce the word *ideology* in a way which may be unfamiliar, associating it with common sense rather than with a set of doctrines or a coherent system of beliefs. My use of the term, derived from Althusser, assumes that ideology is not an optional extra, deliberately adopted by self-conscious individuals ('Conservative party ideology', for instance), but the very condition of our experience of the world, unconscious precisely in that it is unquestioned, taken for granted. Ideology, in Althusser's use of the term, works in conjunction with political practice and economic practice to constitute the *social formation*, a term designed to promote a more complex and radical analysis than the familiar term, 'society', which often evokes either a single homogeneous mass or, alternatively, a loosely connected group of autonomous individuals, and thus offers no challenge to the assumptions of common sense.

Ideology is *inscribed in* language in the sense that it is literally written or spoken in it. Rather than a separate element which exists independently in some free-floating realm of 'ideas' and is subsequently embodied in words, ideology is a way of thinking, speaking, experiencing. These usages will, I hope, become clear and familiar in the course of what follows.

The danger is that their unfamiliar vocabularies render the new theories inaccessible, or not worth the effort of learning to understand them. (Learning theory is much like learning a language.) And, of course, the last resort of common sense is to dismiss as unnecessary 'jargon' any vocabulary which conflicts with its own. This is an effortless way of evading conceptual challenges, of course (and eliciting reassuring sneers), but it negates the repeated liberal-humanist claim to open-mindedness and pluralism. Of course jargon exists, but from a perspective in which ideology is held to be inscribed in language, so that no linguistic forms are ideologically innocent or neutral, it follows that terms cannot be seen as unnecessary simply on the basis that they are new. To resist all linguistic innovation is by implication to claim that we already know all we need to know.

THE PROJECT

In this book I shall try to make the new theories as accessible as possible, without recuperating them for common sense by transcribing them back into the language of every day. The undertaking is in a sense contradictory: to explain is inevitably to reduce the unfamiliarity and so to reduce the extent of the challenge of the post-Saussurean position. On the other hand, I hope that it may prove to be a useful enterprise if it facilitates the reading of the principal theorists themselves.

For this reason, I shall not evade post-Saussurean terminology where it seems to me necessary and, in addition, I shall attempt to show post-Saussurean theory in action, rather than merely to encapsulate in more accessible form a reduced version of the theoretical positions in question. I shall explain those aspects of the theory that seem to me necessary as a basis for a new critical practice, and I shall tend to concentrate on what post-Saussurean theories have in common, rather than on what divides them.

If there is no practice without theory, if common sense presupposes a theoretical basis, however unformulated, it is important to begin by examining some of the propositions of common sense. Thereafter, in chapter 2, I shall give a brief account of the major theoretical assaults on the critical assumptions of common sense which, because they fail to move outside the familiar empiricist-idealist *problematic*, or framework of ideas and concomitant problems, fail to provide a genuinely radical critical theory and practice.

Common sense, then, proposes a *humanism*, based on an *empiricist-idealist* interpretation of the world. In other words, common sense urges that 'man' is the origin and source of meaning, of action and of history (*humanism*). Our concepts and our knowledge are held to be the product of experience (*empiricism*), and this experience is preceded and interpreted by the mind, reason or thought, the property of a transcendent human nature whose essence is the attribute of each individual (*idealism*). These propositions, radically called in question by the implications of post-Saussurean linguistics, constitute the basis of a practice of reading which assumes, whether explicitly or implicitly, the theory of expressive realism. This is the theory that literature reflects the *reality* of experience, as it is perceived by one (especially gifted) individual, who *expresses* this perception in a text which enables other individuals to recognize its truth.

EXPRESSIVE REALISM

Expressive realism belongs roughly to the last two centuries. It coincides, therefore, with the period of industrial capitalism. I shall suggest in chapter 4 that the procedures of expressive realism have certain ideological implications which may indicate that their development during this period is in practice more than coincidental.

In the mean time, in order to come to terms with expressive realism, it might be helpful to find a clear and explicit formulation of the position which is still so widely taken for granted. Definitions of commonsense positions are found most often in periods when the position in question is new, and in the process of displacing an earlier position, or when it is under attack. At times when the same position is widely shared, its principles are more commonly implicit than explicit. The Aristotelean concept of art as mimesis, the imitation of reality, was widely current throughout the early modern period and during the eighteenth century. Expressive realism resulted from the fusion of this concept with the new Romantic conviction that poetry, as 'the spontaneous overflow of powerful feelings', *expressed* the perceptions and emotions of a person 'possessed of more than usual organic sensibility' (Wordsworth 1974, 1: 126).

By the mid-nineteenth century the expressive-realist theory had become widely established in relation to literature, but painting, and particularly landscape painting, found its first major post-Romantic theorist in John Ruskin. When, in *Modern Painters* in the 1840s, Ruskin set out to defend landscape painting in general, and the paintings of J. M. W. Turner in particular, he did so by invoking in relation to the visual arts the theory already widely current in discussions of poetry. He uses, he says, 'the words painter and poet quite indifferently' (Ruskin 1903–12, 5: 221), 'treating poetry and painting as synonymous' (3: 88). His account of the landscape painter's obligations offers, therefore, a particularly clear and striking formulation of a position which was then relatively new and to some degree embattled (3: 133–9). Ruskin insists that

the landscape painter must always have two great and distinct ends: the first, to induce in the spectator's mind the faithful conception of any natural objects whatsoever; the second, to guide the spectator's mind to those objects most worthy of its contemplation, and to inform him of the thoughts and feelings with which these were regarded by the artist himself.

In other words, the artist must both represent (re-present) faithfully the objects portrayed, and express the thoughts and feelings they evoke in him or her. There is no doubt, in Ruskin's view, that the second aim is the more important, because it leaves the spectator more than delighted –

ennobled and instructed, under the sense of having not only beheld a new scene, but of having held communion with a new mind, and having been endowed for a time with the keen perception and the impetuous emotion of a nobler and more penetrating intelligence.

But this creates a difficulty. Whereas truth to nature is universally pleasing – the representational aspects of art will delight everyone – the expressive aspects are apparent only to the few, 'can only be met and understood by persons having some sort of sympathy with the high and solitary minds which produced it – sympathy only to be felt by minds in some degree high and solitary themselves'. To avoid this difficulty, Ruskin's criticism will concentrate first on the question of truth to nature, since,

although it is possible to reach what I have stated to be the first end of art, the representation of facts, without reaching the second, the representation of thoughts, yet it is altogether impossible to reach the second without having previously reached the first.

Mimetic accuracy is the foundation of all art: 'nothing can atone for the want of truth'; 'no artist can be graceful, imaginative, or original, unless he be truthful'. And so, in the first instance, 'I shall look only for truth; bare, clear, downright statement of facts; showing in each particular, as far as I am able, what the truth of nature is, and then seeking for the plain expression of it'. Art is mimetic and expressive, and Ruskin goes on to argue that the two qualities are, in fact, not two but one. In portraying the truth, the artist expresses a personal and particularly incisive perception of that truth.

It is worth noting that for Ruskin the world of natural objects, of bare, clear, downright facts, is unproblematically given, accessible to experience, and able to be re-presented in art. Equally, the mind of the spectator and the (nobler and more penetrating) mind of the artist are ready to perceive these natural objects. Already, however, Ruskin glimpses a problem in his empiricist-idealist position. The facts of nature are there for everyone to see and to be plainly represented; some people (high and solitary minds) perceive these facts more keenly and, if they are artists, portray them invested with a nobility not apparent to everyone, or in other words, represent them *differently*. This representation, however, is also accurate. But instead of pursuing the implications of this recognition that the world may be perceived and represented in different ways, without either way being simply false, and that, like nature, the work of art too may be read in different ways by different spectators, Ruskin falls back on an uneasy separation of 'the representation of facts' from 'the representation of thoughts'.

By the 1960s, well over a century later, expressive realism had been subjected to a series of theoretical attacks, not only from the Russian formalists, whose work was then relatively little known in the West, and the Prague semioticians, who at that time appeared very esoteric indeed, but also by the New Critics and Northrop Frye, both powerful influences within the Anglo-American tradition. In Barbara Hardy's discussion, first published in 1964, of the proper place of form in criticism, the expressive-realist presuppositions are, in consequence, newly articulated, but now with a certain defensive edge:

> The novelist, whoever he is and wherever he is writing, is giving form to a story, giving form to his moral and metaphysical views, and giving form to his particular experience of sensations, people, places, and society.
>
> (Hardy 1964: 1)

These practices, the sentence proposes, define the essential work of the novelist, independent of time or place. That such practices might in themselves be ideological, and thus characteristic of a particular period of history, is not suggested. Ideology is mentioned elsewhere, but is understood as 'simplification or distortion', a deviation from 'truthfulness', the product of an individual 'error or a partiality or a blindness or a fantasy which may be transferred from life to art' (6). Such distortions, Barnara Hardy claims, mar the work of Daniel Defoe, Thomas Hardy and, occasionally, D. H. Lawrence.

The statement I have quoted, however apparently innocent, depends on certain quite specific assumptions. It assumes the existence of a story, views and experiences in the mind of the novelist, prior to and independent of the formulation of them. These pre-exist the narrative and are given form in it. Narrative form, it is argued, comprises a story, an argument or moral theme and the imitation of experience, while the methodological separation of these three is, in a sense, artificial, since the story embodies the conjunction of 'truthful realization' and 'morality', the novelist's 'evaluation of life' (2–3). The values Barbara Hardy defends emerge very clearly in her vocabulary of relative admiration and dispraise: richness, honesty, immediacy are contrasted with schematism, implausibility and, of course, ideology. And in case we are tempted to attribute undue value to perfection of form, we are reminded of the real criteria for judging the novel, apparently on the assumption that, in these extreme cases at least, we share the conclusion of the argument because it is 'obvious':

> If we admire the narrative curve of tension we may place Trollope higher than Tolstoy. If we admire the thematic organization we may place James Gould Cozzens higher than Lawrence. If we admire the form of truth, we can do neither. (4)

During the period of just over a century which lies between the two critics I have quoted, expressive realism appears more commonly in terms of a set of shared assumptions, rather than as a position to be explicitly defended. In the version which is inscribed in much of the critical writing of F. R. Leavis, for instance, it is not identified as theory. Indeed, Leavis deplored theory. The task of the critic, he argued, is to develop an ever finer response to the concrete experience that is given in the text, and not to tangle with abstract theoretical issues, for fear of blunting the edge of this response (Leavis 1976: 213).

But Leavis's own critical writings themselves demonstrate that there is no practice without theory. In 'Henry James and the Function of Criticism', for instance, Leavis grounds his discussion of what he finds most valuable in James's work on uninterrogated expressive-realist presuppositions. The novels he most admires are praised for 'the vivid concreteness of the rendering of this world of individual centres of consciousness we live in' (231), and this in turn is derived from James's own 'most vital experience' (228). The values embodied in his novels express James's profound personal preoccupation with – and fear of missing – the full experience of life. The concept presented in his work of a possible 'civilization', both spiritual and external, is seen as directly and unproblematically related to his way of life, and his literary failures are the result of a 'malnutrition' of his own 'deep centre' of consciousness: 'James paid the penalty of living too much as a novelist, and not richly enough as a man . . .' (228). Author and text are inextricably intertwined, to the point where James's literary inadequacies are interpreted as a direct expression of his personal inadequacies.

Indeed, in Leavis's criticism in general a recurring slippage from text to author manifests itself in a characteristic way of formulating his observations. In the following quotations, isolated from their contexts, it is true, it can be seen that the text has diappeared entirely, leaving the assumption, not unfamiliar from commonsense accounts of the nature of communication, that writing is intelligible primarily as a revelation of the qualities of mind of its indivdual author or speaker:

> There is no profound emotional disorder in Lawrence, no obdurate major disharmony; intelligence in him can be, as it is, the servant of the whole integrated psyche. It is the representative in consciousness of the complex need of the whole being, and is not thwarted or disabled by inner contradictions in him, whether we have him as artist, critic, or expositor.

> (Leavis 1973: 29)

On Swift:

> He was, in various ways, curiously unaware – the reverse of clairvoyant. He is distinguished by the intensity of his feelings, not by

> insight into them, and he certainly does not impress us as a mind in
> possession of its experience.
>
> (Leavis 1976: 87)

And on the novelists of *The Great Tradition*: 'They are all distinguished by a vital capacity for experience, a kind of reverent openness before life, and a marked moral intensity'. (Leavis 1962: 17)

Meanwhile, the assumptions of expressive realism are still perpetuated in the observations and practices of some writers, reviewers, and even English departments – though not, of course, unchallenged by alternative theories and practices. Until recently, literature has been widely treated as a reflection of life. In Iris Murdoch's view, 'bad art is a lie about the world, and what is by contrast seen as good is in some important evident sense seen as *ipso facto* true and as expressive of reality' (Murdoch 1977: 83). The novel, above all, is praised for its 'authenticity' in describing the world of social relationships, or conveying the inner experience (sometimes seen as 'universal') of the individual in quest of identity.

The expressive attitude, too, is still to be found, taken for granted in popular criticism. 'What is he trying to tell us?', 'what does she mean in this passage?' The text is regarded as a way of arriving at something anterior to it: the convictions of the author, or his or her experience as part of that society at that particular time. To understand the text is to explain it, it would seem, in terms of the author's ideas, psychological state or social background. Books about authors often begin with a brief biography, discussing the influence of the family, the environment or the society. The commonest way of writing about literature has been, until recently, to write a book about an author, analysing his or her works chronologically to show the developing skill with which the author's developing insights are *expressed*. And in English departments essays and examinations answers are commonly written about an author – either the whole *oeuvre* or selected works. The implication is that one of a writer's works necessarily illuminates the others, *expressing* comparable themes or attitudes.

Just as for Ruskin, the mimetic and the expressive are one. If, on the one hand, for Leavis it is the writer's intuitive apprehension of 'felt life' that makes him or her great, for Lukács, in many ways at the opposite theoretical extreme, what makes a writer great is 'sympathy with the sufferings of the people', in conjunction with a 'thirst for truth', a 'fanatic striving for reality' (Lukács 1950: 11–12).

On the other hand, the expressive-realist position has been subject to a series of challenges, and in some cases by theories which have since become orthodoxies in their own right. In this way, it has become apparent that expressive realism presents a number of problems not easily resolved within the framework of common sense. Difficulties that have emerged include the problem of access to the idea or experience which is held to precede the expression of it. What form does it take? Do ideas exist outside their formulation? Is the idea formulated in one piece of writing (a letter or a diary) *the same* as an idea formulated *in different words* in another (a literary text)?

Further, what do we mean by 'realism'? In what sense is fiction 'true'? What is the relationship between a text (a discursive construct) and the world? To what extent is it possible to perceive the world independently of the conventional ways in which it is represented? To what extent is experience contained by language, society, history?

In the next chapter I shall discuss some of the more influential twentieth-century challenges to expressive realism, and the theoretical problems they in turn raised in the process of putting forward alternatives. I shall suggest that, in so far as these theoretical challenges failed to break with the empiricist-idealist problematic, their effects were contradictory, liberating new ways of approaching literary texts, but failing to construct a genuinely alternative and radical critical practice.

2

CHALLENGES TO EXPRESSIVE REALISM

NEW CRITICISM

One of the most important assaults on the orthodoxy of expressive realism was the work in the 1940s and 1950s of the American New Critics, John Crowe Ransom, Cleanth Brooks, W. K. Wimsatt and others, whose position in turn owed a good deal to the writings of T. S. Eliot and I. A. Richards. In 'The Intentional Fallacy', first published in 1946, Wimsatt, working in conjunction with Monroe C. Beardsley, delivered a resounding blow to the expressive theory by arguing that the quest for the author's intentions had nothing to do with literary criticism.

The intentionalist position, Wimsatt and Beardsley declared (and the essay has a certain declaratory quality, presenting itself as a New Critical manifesto) was a Romantic fallacy, consistent only with the conviction that poetry is to be approached as the efflux of a noble soul. Knowledge of the author's intentions was 'neither available nor desirable' (Wimsatt 1970: 3). The intentions of the author were not to be found outside the text in biographies or in history; where they seemed to be available – in direct statements by the author, for instance – they could not be taken at their face value; and where a knowledge of the intention was assumed by the reader or critic it was likely to mislead. Further, the pursuit of 'sincerity', 'spontaneity', 'authenticity' and the other expressive values associated with intentionalism had no relation to the more precise and truly critical values of 'integrity', 'unity', 'maturity' and 'subtlety' (9). The latter were properties not of the author but of the text.

Despite a protracted and vigorous controversy, continuing well into the 1970s (and helpfully reprinted in David Newton-de Molina's *On Literary Intention*), the expressive theory in its simple form never fully recovered from the attack of Wimsatt and Beardsley. Their New Critical insistence on the words of the text became an orthodoxy in its turn, and in English departments, if not in the world at large, the search for something anterior to the text, empirical evidence of a specific purpose in the author's mind, became rarer, normally calling for some form of apology.

What survived, however, was a kind of implicit intentionalism, a quest for what it *appeared* the author had had in mind on the evidence of the text itself, and here it seems that Wimsatt and Beardsley had themselves left open this possibility: 'If the poet succeeded in doing it, then the poem itself shows what he was trying to do' (Wimsatt 1970: 4). In this way the poem can still be seen as a means of discovering the intentions of an individual, even if it is not immediately clear which poems can be said to succeed in these terms. It was therefore possible to adopt the New Critical position and share the rejection of intentionalism without fully confronting the idealist assumption that the text constituted an expression of an idea, a presence which existed in some shadowy realm of subjectivity anterior to and independent of the text itself.

The importance of 'The Intentional Fallacy' lies, however, in its uncertainties at least as much as in its declarations. There is clear evidence of an attempt to come to grips with the problem of the author's authority over the text, with the concept of meaning as prior to expression, which confines the text for all time to a single and univocal reading located somewhere other than on the printed page. Wimsatt and Beardsley effectively begin the process of prising the text away from the author, even if their formulation of their own position is an uneasy one:

> The poem is not the critic's own and not the author's (it is detached
> from the author at birth and goes about the world beyond his power to
> intend about it or control it). The poem belongs to the public. It is
> embodied in language, the peculiar possession of the public, and it is
> about the human being, an object of public knowledge. What is said
> about the poem is subject to the same scrutiny as any statement in
> linguistics or in the general science of psychology.
>
> (5)

The concept of the text as belonging to the public, because language is
public, marks a significant departure from the expressive theory, even
though in this formulation it is not entirely clear precisely how the
concept is to be understood. The New Critics never fully succeeded in
theorizing the relationship between the poem made of words, the
verbal icon, and the language within which it exists and signifies, and
for this reason their practice never fully realized the potential implicit
in their position. They consistently urged that there was no distinction between form and content, that texts cannot be understood as
ideas wrapped in emotions, or meanings decorated with imagery,
and in this context Cleanth Brooks in 'The Heresy of Paraphrase'
quotes with approval W. M. Urban's observation: 'The artist does not
first intuit his object and then find the appropriate medium. It is
rather in and through his medium that he intuits the object' (Brooks
1968: 163).

In this essay Brooks seems to glimpse the fact that it is language itself
which offers the possibility of meaning, and if it were not for the New
Critical rejection of all interest in the process of reading, he might have
gone on to propose that the reader's experience is made possible by the
text itself. In a sense the New Critics always perceived something of this
kind.[1] In the same essay Brooks again introduces a formula which
seems to urge that the poem is not a secondary transcription into
words of a prior event: 'The poem, if it be a true poem is a simulacrum
of reality . . . by being an experience rather than any mere statement
about experience or any mere abstraction from experience' (173). It
was on this basis that the New Critics consistently demanded a close
and detailed attention to the formal properties of the text. The invisible
thread linking two minds which defines the text in the expressive

theory had become visible, discursive, subject to 'objective' and public scrutiny.

The major theoretical difficulty in the New Critical position was the problem of meaning. Within the expressive theory the text could be seen to possess a single, determinate meaning, however complex, and the authority for this meaning was the author. Meaning was what the author put into the text. More recent theorists, having rejected as inaccessible the author's intention as the guarantee of meaning, have constituted the reader as a new authority for the single and univocal meaning of the text. The New Critics firmly rejected both these possi-bilities and were left with the unsatisfactory concept of meaning existing 'on the page':

> We enquire now not about origins, nor about effects, but about the work so far as it can be considered by itself as a body of meaning. Neither the qualities of the author's mind nor the effects of a poem upon a reader's mind should be confused with the moral quality of the meaning expressed by the poem itself.
>
> (Wimsatt 1970: 87)

This is a clear rejection of the idealist notion that meaning floats in some extra-symbolic realm, independent of language, in people's minds. But the continued assumption that meaning is single, and the continued quest for a guarantee of this single meaning results in a conviction that the meaning of any text is timeless, universal and trans-historical: 'though cultures have changed and will change, poems remain and explain' (39).

The New Critics have repeatedly been accused of being ahistorical or anti-historical, but strictly speaking this accusation is not well founded. Many of their individual readings are quite adequately historical in the traditional sense of being well-informed and scholarly. The problem is a more fundamental one, namely, the failure to recognize that meaning exists only within a specific language, or more precisely within a spe-cific culture, and that it cannot therefore inhere timelessly within the words on the page. The historical approach to literature recognizes this problem and deals with it coherently, if narrowly: *Paradise Lost* 'means' whatever *Paradise Lost* appears to have offered as the position from which it was intelligible to its earliest readers. The expressive theory maintains that *Paradise Lost* 'means' whatever Milton 'had in mind' as its meaning when he composed it. But New Criticism is compelled by its own logic to argue that the text simply 'means' in isolation, and means now what it has always meant, that the poem is a 'concrete universal', the individual instance of an eternally and universally intelligible verity.

This in turn forces the New Critics back again, well away from the frontiers they seemed to have approached in their insistence on the public ownership of the text. If meaning is made possible by language, and language changes, meaning must be subject to change. In order to arrest the flux of meaning, to fix the single position of intelligibility of the text, the New Critics are forced back on a naive empiricism-idealism which maintains that words stand either for things or for experiences, and that these inhere timelessly in the phenomenal world or in the continuity of essential human nature. Thus history becomes an anticipation of the present in all important aspects, and the specific, ideologically constructed experience of the twentieth century is universalized as the unchanging natural order:

> No amount of deference paid to history can escape the fact that every explanation of a word is in the end an appeal to things, or the companion fact that old documents are mediated in the direction of things by new documents. 'For myself,' says a distinguished Shakespearean editor, 'I have learnt more about Shakespeare's Henry from Wavell's *Life of Allenby* than from all the critics put together.' To understand the heroism of Henry or the irony of Pope and Dryden we have to draw upon historical information and linguistic glosses. But we have to draw equally upon the modern world and our own experience. We find the meaning of heroism and of irony ultimately in the objects of our own experience and in our own minds.
>
> (Wimsatt 1970: 255)

The weakness of the theory originates in the attempt to locate meaning in a single place, in the words of the text, 'on the page'. In practice, texts do offer positions from which they are intelligible, but these positions are never single. It is language which provides the possibility of meaning, but because language is not static but perpetually in process, what is inherent in the text is a range of possibilities of meaning. Texts, in other words, are plural, open to a number of interpretations. Meanings are not fixed or given, but are released in the process of reading, and criticism is concerned with the range of possible readings.

Literature for the New Critics is still concerned with truth, though it is a truth more complex, more paradoxical, more mysterious than the truths of every day. It is the truth of unchanging experience in all its complexity and ambiguity, which the poem as icon 'embodies in language' and offers for contemplation. This contemplation, performed in isolation, involves only the individual reader and the individual text. The poem, self-contained and closed, constitutes a pattern of knowledge which leads to a philosophy of detachment. Rising above the vicissitudes of the world, 'poems remain and explain', and New Critical readers encounter in solitude the paradoxes of human experience which lead to a wise passiveness.[2]

New Criticism thus constitutes a contradictory moment, in a sense a liberation from the authoritarianism of the expressive theory, but inhibited from taking advantage of this liberation by its own commitment to empiricism and a concomitant idealism. Unable to place its own perceptions in the framework of an adequate theory, New Criticism remained fundamentally non-theoretical and non-explanatory. Asserting that objective analysis of form is the task of criticism, it failed to pursue the theoretical implications of this position by developing an analysis of the relations between language and meaning. Cutting itself off from all textuality except the poetic, it increasingly isolated literary criticism from other concerns. As a result, it gradually became an increasingly over-ingenious and sterile quest for complexities and ambiguities, so that by 1961 René Wellek, though declaring himself basically in sympathy with its aims, observed that New Criticism had 'not been able to avoid the dangers of ossification and mechanical imitation. There seems time for a change.' (Wellek 1963: 360).[3]

NORTHROP FRYE

New Criticism assumed the possibility of an 'innocent' reading, a confrontation with the words on the page unmediated by the experience of other texts. In other words, it ignored the intertextual elements of intelligibility, the recognition of similarities and differences between a text and all the other texts we have read, a growing 'knowledge' which enables us to identify a story as this story, and indeed to know it to be a story at all, or which makes it possible to understand one poem as a lyric, another as an epic, with all the expectations and assumptions that that understanding entails. The 'structuralism' of Northrop Frye constituted a reaction against some of the central convictions of New Criticism, first in its insistence on literary criticism as a discipline which is not merely parasitic on literary texts themselves, and second in its concomitant quest for a poetics, a systematic framework within which to order our knowledge of literature and our critical procedures.

Existing criticism, Frye argues, is without system, atomistic, intuitive and so finally élitist, a ritual of sensibility which mystifies the possession of an illusory 'good taste'. In place of this 'mystery-religion without a gospel', he proposes that criticism should become 'a coherent and systematic study, the elementary principles of which could be explained to any intelligent nineteen-year-old' (Frye 1957: 14). He points out that we have no clear answer to the question, 'what is literature?', that we have no single word for a literary text, no theoretical analysis of the distinction between prose and verse, and no way at all of classifying prose forms (12–14). What follows in the *Anatomy of Criticism* is designed to provide the critic with a system of classification of modes, symbols, mythic structures and genres, facilitating the making of distinctions and comparisons across the traditional boundaries between authors or between narrowly defined historical periods.

It is an ambitious project, but supported by Frye's wide range of reading, his fluency and his wit, it succeeds dazzlingly. The *Anatomy of Criticism* is an authoritative – and liberating – work. In these circumstances it seems ungracious to complain that Frye's theory is finally unable to solve precisely the problems confronted by the New Critics.

Ostensibly Frye's position is fundamentally antithetical to that of the New Critics. Where they are atomistic and detailed, he is categorical and sweeping; where they are Aristotelian, he is Neoplatonic, seeing literature as realizing a potential golden world rather than imitating a brazen one. Literature is not a means of access to solid things and unmediated experiences, but constitutes a realm of 'autonomous culture', which he defines as 'the total body of imaginative hypothesis in a society and its tradition' (127).

Frye views the quest for realism in literature with distaste, to the point where any work with 'a controlling aim of descriptive accuracy' is by definition non-literary (75). He equates literature with fiction and dismisses any objections that this excludes Pope's *Essay on Man* (or Wordsworth, or Gibbon) on the grounds that to read these works as literature is to read them for their style rather than their subject matter (85). He does not deny that literary texts have meaning, but he insists that their final direction of meaning is 'inward', 'centripetal' rather than 'centrifugal'. Literature is formal, not instrumental, and any text which is primarily about the world is simply not literature:

> In literature, questions of fact or truth are subordinated to the primary literary aims of producing a structure of words for its own sake, and the sign-values of symbols are subordinated to their importance as a structure of interconnected motifs. Wherever we have an autonomous verbal structure of this kind, we have literature. Wherever this autonomous structure is lacking, we have language, words used instrumentally to help human consciousness do or understand something else.

(74)

The criterion of realism is conventional, more a matter of the familiarity of the form of representation than of content (132).

The writer's intention is also purely formal – to produce a structure of words for its own sake – and this puts paid to the expressive theory. In an essay on *Lycidas* Frye entertainingly proposes that the poem is 'passionately sincere', 'because Milton was deeply interested in the structure and symbolism of funeral elegies, and had been practising since adolescence on every fresh corpse in sight, from the university beadle to the fair infant dying of a cough' (Frye 1972: 438).

Frye's formalism is not entirely pure, however. He describes his own procedure as 'archetypal criticism', and defines 'archetypes' as recurring images or symbols which connect one text with another and constitute a source of the intelligibility of the text. It is not the content of the quest-motif that matters, or the meaning of the myth of rebirth in spring, but the fact that these ritual patterns inform text after text in societies remote from each other and from the primitive. But it emerges that the archetypal critic, though not concerned with the historical origins of the myth, nonetheless finds its origins, not this time in experience but in 'desire'. The archetypes recur not because they are true but because they are universally the best way of holding an audience's attention (Frye 1957: 109), and this in turn is because they represent what is desired and the obstacles to what is desired, the deepest wishes and anxieties of humanity (104–6).

Underlying Frye's formalism, therefore, is a concept of human nature and of culture which sees literature as imitating not the world but rather 'the total dream of man' (119). Civilization, he argues, is the process of producing human forms (gardens, architecture, society) out of nature, and this civilization, the goal of human work, is born of desire. Literature both shows and embodies this goal but, read 'anagogically', it does more, not merely transcending nature but containing it:

> Nature is now inside the mind of an infinite man who builds his cities out of the Milky Way. This is not reality, but it is the conceivable or imaginative limit of desire, which is infinite, eternal, and hence apocalyptic.
>
> (119)

Literature constitutes its own independent universe, in relation to which 'life' is no more than 'a vast mass of potential literary forms' (122).

Many admirers of Frye have made use of his categories and ignored or rejected his conceptions of humanity and of culture, but to do so is to ignore the elements which hold the theory together. Any archetypal theory or system of classification must rest on similar assumptions, even if they remain unstated. For Frye the archetypes recur because human nature is constant, not just in its physical needs but in its desire for the forms of civilization, its rage for order in the face of chaos. Literature is the autonomous embodiment of this order, its modes (mythic, romantic, mimetic and ironic) manifold but recurring in cycles, its essential structures ultimately reducible to the duality of desire and anxiety.

Paradoxically, then, although Frye seems to start from a position antithetical to that of the New Critics, he finally arrives at a very similar one, in which literature transcends history and ideology, giving expression to the timeless aspirations of an essentially unchanging human nature. He echoes (though with a slightly different emphasis) Wimsatt's statement that the text is intelligible in terms of history and the modern world simultaneously (51), and he even lends the dignity (and *naturalness*) of universality to the specifically bourgeois myth which equates social integration with economic success:

> Domestic comedy is usually based on the Cinderella archetype, the kind of thing that happens when Pamela's virtue is rewarded, the incorporation of an individual very like the reader into the society aspired to by both, a society ushered in with a happy rustle of bridal gowns and banknotes.

> (44)

It is not, therefore, surprising to find that Frye's theory of language is not radically different from the New Critical theory, and participates in some of the same uncertainties. His formalism implies a certain attention to the language of literary works, and indeed at moments – in the essay on 'Rhetorical Criticism' in the *Anatomy*, for instance – he seems to concede that the reader's response is rooted in the words of the text. But in general words are symbols for things (73) or thoughts (83),[4] and it appears that textuality is a secondary order, which merely 'imitates' the world of ideas. Thus, for instance, although there are problems of translation, especially between languages 'in different cultural orbits', none the less 'it seems clear that we can eventually, with patient and sympathetic study, find out what is going on in a Polynesian or Iroquois mind' (333). Thought takes place independently of language, in the mind, and meaning precedes its expression in words.

> For it is clear that all verbal structures with meaning are verbal imitations of that elusive psychological and physiological process known as thought, a process stumbling through emotional entanglements,

sudden irrational convictions, involuntary gleams of insight, rational-
ized prejudices, and blocks of panic and inertia, finally to reach a
completely incommunicable intuition. Anyone who imagines that
philosophy is not a verbal imitation of this process, but the process
itself, has clearly not done much thinking.

(83)

Here the individual experience of thinking, 'how it feels', is presented
as the ultimate evidence for the nature of thought.

But as I hope Chapter 3 will make clear, language is not an imitation
of thought, but its condition. It is only within language that the production of meaning is possible, however much our individual experience of producing meaning is one of stumbling and panic, and of
looking for adequate formulations of what seems intuitive. Of course,
it is true that the written text does not necessarily reproduce the empirical process of thinking, but our analysis of the nature of thought need
not confine itself to the question of how it feels to think.

Frye's final appeal to experience, in conjunction with his account of
a thought process culminating in 'a completely incommunicable intuition', places him within the same empiricist-idealist problematic as
the New Critics. And for all its claims to science and systematicity, his
own theory, like theirs, is fundamentally non-explanatory. Meaning for
Frye inheres timelessly in 'verbal structures', intuitively available to
readers in quite different ages and places, because they recognize in
them the echo of their own wishes and anxieties. But the only evidence
for this concept of an essentially unchanging human nature is precisely
the body of literary texts which the concept apparently offers to
explain. The relationship between desire and language and between
language and meaning is not discussed.

At the same time, Frye's theory is to some degree contradictory. His
own experience must have shown that his students, for instance, did
not intuitively recognize in *Lycidas* the archetypal figures of Adonis,
Orpheus and the dying god of vegetation myth and, as Frye himself
concedes, it is only for 'the properly instructed reader' that the classical
references in Yeats's 'Leda' or Eliot's 'Sweeney Among the Night-
ingales' have 'as much cumulative power as ever' (102). Here Frye,
like the New Critics, seems to glimpse the fact that meaning is

conventional, a matter of familiarity rather than intuition. This recognition of intertextuality (reference to other texts) as a source of intelligibility, like the New Critical concept of the text as public, is a radical development which is thwarted by its context in the theoretical structure as a whole. The Anglo-American tradition of critical theory begins to appear as a series of such developments, based on a recognition of the inadequacies of the commonsense account of literature, but unable to resolve the problems it presents from within the empiricist-idealist conceptual framework. What is needed is a fundamental break with the empiricist-idealist position.

A similar radicalism, similarly inhibited, appears in Frye's recurrent glimpses of the plurality of meaning. His impatient rejection of the invocation of the author as guarantee of the single meaning of the text is worth quoting in full:

> criticism, if a science, must be totally intelligible, but literature, as the order of words which makes the science possible, is, so far as we know, an inexhaustible source of new critical discoveries, and would be even if new works of literature ceased to be written. If so, then the search for a limiting principle in literature in order to discourage the development of criticism is mistaken. The absurd quantum formula of criticism, the assertion that the critic should confine himself to 'getting out' of a poem exactly what the poet may vaguely be assumed to have been aware of 'putting in', is one of the many slovenly illiteracies that the absence of systematic criticism has allowed to grow up. This quantum theory is the literary form of what may be called the fallacy of premature teleology. It corresponds, in the natural sciences, to the assertion that a phenomenon is as it is because Providence in its inscrutable wisdom made it so. That is, the critic is assumed to have no conceptual framework: it is simply his job to take a poem into which a poet has diligently stuffed a specific number of beauties or effects, and complacently extract them one by one, like his prototype Little Jack Horner.

(17–18)

Frye thus goes beyond the New Critics in rejecting entirely the quest for even implicit intention. Freed in this way from the tyranny of the author, and available for interpretation by a self-conscious and systematic criticism which is independent of literature, the text is inevitably plural, open to a number of readings. The evidence for its plurality, Frye argues, is the simultaneous development of a number of schools of critical theory, each emphasizing different elements in the text, each discovering distinct patterns of significance. To opt for a single pattern is to narrow the possibilities arbitrarily and unnecessarily. Critical commentary cannot exhaust the potential meanings of the text, but rather tends to isolate the aspects of its meaning which are intelligible or valuable to certain readers at certain times (87).

It is disappointing, therefore, to discover that this rich plurality is destined to be contained within a repressive pluralism which argues that conflict between points of view only inhibits the advancement of learning. For such a polemical critic, Frye is curiously antipathetic to the notion that contention can be productive. Ultimately, he urges, the plural meanings of the text are not in conflict with one another but complementary, each contributing to our understanding of the work as a (single) whole. We may stand close to the text or further back from it, and at any distance we may see different elements of its total organization. Similarly, distinct critical procedures are most fruitfully seen as contributing to a cumulative and finally comprehensive understanding, offering a series of contexts in which to place the totality of the work. Frye's object, then, is not to exclude any critical approach, but to break down barriers between approaches (341).

It must be said that this position is undermined, if not contradicted, by Frye's own scathing rejection of the specific critical approach which I have identified as expressive realism. But if it is inconsistent with elements of the *Anatomy* (which is large and contains multitudes), the position is perfectly consistent with Frye's conception, inherited from Matthew Arnold, of the social function of literature. Society, like critical theory, is riddled with conflicts, and particularly class conflicts. Literary criticism, as part of a liberal education, can make it possible to conceive of a free and classless society, transcending the world we know, 'clear of the bondage of history' (347). Thus criticism, autonomous and isolated, acts as a solvent for the class struggle, not in the world but in the imagination.[5]

These are finally the fruits of Frye's liberal humanism, which is founded in turn on empiricism-idealism. The human mind, forever isolated from the social formation in which in practice it is constructed, is seen as unable to influence the course of history in any substantial way. Less optimistic than Arnold about the power of education, Frye, like the New Critics, is left with the detachment which constitutes 'intellectual freedom' as his highest social value (348).

This in itself provides a refutation of his own arguments for the autonomy of criticism. No theoretical position can exist in isolation: any conceptual framework for literary criticism has implications which stretch beyond criticism itself to ideology and the place of ideology in the social formation as a whole. Assumptions about literature involve assumptions about language and about meaning, and these in turn involve assumptions about human society. The independent universe of literature and the autonomy of criticism are illusory.

READER-POWER

Among the more recent challenges to expressive realism, probably one of the most interesting is the assertion of the role of the reader in relation to the literary text. At its best, interest in the reader is entirely liberating, a rejection of authorial tyranny in favour of the participation of readers in the production of a plurality of meanings; at its worst, reader-theory merely constructs a new authority-figure as guarantor of a single meaning, a timeless, transcendent, highly trained model reader who cannot be wrong. Most practising reader-theorists operate between these extremes and encounter, implicitly or explicitly, a number of theoretical problems in the process.

Walter J. Slatoff's *With Respect to Readers* manifests a number of these. Slatoff's important discovery is that texts cannot determine across history and for all readers how they are to be read. The formal properties of the work cannot ensure identical interpretations and responses but in practice leave readers a good deal of freedom to produce meanings. Unfortunately, however, Slatoff locates the differences in the empiricist-idealist (and non-explanatory) concept of each individual's unique 'nature, experience, training, temperament, values, biases, or motive for reading' (Slatoff 1970: 35), rather than in an analysis of discursive and ideological differences. For this reason he is able to slide easily into the notion that 'most readers' do in fact succeed in arriving at a practice which he identifies as 'good reading' (25), and they do so by rejecting readings which are 'clearly inappropriate' (78) in favour of 'sympathy' or 'empathy' with what finally turns out to have been the intention of the 'implied author', the 'human presence' in the work.

The concept of the implied author, originally invoked by Wayne Booth in *The Rhetoric of Fiction* as a concession to the arguments against the quest for the intentions of the empirical author, is an extremely useful instrument in the formal analysis of narrative texts. It designates the implicit 'speaker' in the novel, for instance, the teller of the story as a whole, who is different from the implied authors of other stories (Booth 1961: 70–1). In recent French criticism it is common to make a distinction between this implied narrator of the story as a whole, the 'subject of the enunciation', and the 'subjects of the *énoncé*', who are characters (including fictional narrators) with their own subordinate utterances:

> The narrator is the subject of the enunciation represented by a book. . . . It is he or she who places certain descriptions before others, although these preceded them in the chronology of the story. It is he or she who makes us see the action through the eyes of this or that character, or indeed through his or her own eyes . . .
>
> (Todorov 1966: 146)

Todorov insists on the formal distinction between

> the two aspects of the *énoncé* which are always present: its double nature of *énoncé* and *énonciation*. These two aspects give life to two equally linguistic realities, that of the characters and that of the narrator-listener duality. . . . The individual who says *I* in a novel is not the *I* of the discourse, otherwise called the subject of the *énonciation*. He is only a character. . . . But there exists another *I*, an *I* for the most part invisible, which refers to the narrator, the 'poetic personality' which we apprehend through the discourse.
>
> (Todorov 1970: 132)

I hope to be able to return to this distinction in order to illustrate its usefulness as an instrument of formal analysis in Chapter 4.

In Slatoff's version, however, the implied author is not a formal concept in quite this way. On the contrary, he or she is not in practice readily distinguishable from an empirical author, whose qualities of mind are the source of the value of the text. Thus he alludes to 'George Eliot's earnestness', 'the smugness of Thackeray' and 'the clumsy sincerity of Dreiser' in a way that suggests only a very narrow gap between his own position and the expressive theory (Slatoff 1970: 127). The authoritarianism of this stance manifests itself in the terms Slatoff employs to define the practices of 'good readers and critics' (112), who learn to 'submit' to the work and let their 'responses' be 'directed and limited' by it (35). Readings which manifest a 'lack of harmony' between reader and writer (readings, presumably, which are not properly 'submissive') are identified as 'maladjustments' (71 ff). Thus Slatoff's admiration for 'open' texts, works which are disruptive or disturbing, rather than ordered and harmonious, though it comes close to recognizing the possibility that texts might challenge convention by involving the reader in contradiction, finally slides disappointingly back into a conventional respect for texts as authorial soliloquies, manifestations of subjective conflict and irresolution in the (implied?) author.

In addition to the by now familiar empiricist-idealist suppression of language, Slatoff is also inhibited from taking advantage of the radical possibilities of his position by the presupposition that the reading practice and the 'emotional response as he calls it, of 'most' readers is simply given, *natural* and therefore impassable. Any other way of reading is either, 'inappropriate' or, worse, 'deeply conditioned' (93). His theoretical basis, therefore, is once again the communication model of common sense, in which the text is an invisible thread connecting two consciousnesses. The production of meaning by the reader is thus essentially a movement by the reader along this thread towards the position of the author. What is lacking from Slatoff's analysis is any concept of the role of assumptions and expectations in the production of meaning. If what we look for is the 'human presence' in the work, that is what we shall find. But to confine ourselves to that quest is tantamount to reading in (ideological) blinkers.

German reception theory, (*Rezeptionsästhetik*, the Aesthetics of Reception), on the other hand, adopts a more sophisticated attitude to theory and to history. As Hans Robert Jauss insists, 'a literary work is not an object which stands by itself and which offers the same face to each reader in each period. It is not a monument which reveals its timeless essence in a monologue' (Jauss 1974: 14). The history of the reception of literary texts is concerned precisely with the problem of how we can account for differences of reading in terms of the intertextual and historical expectations of readers. It is a procedure which 'brings out the hermeneutic difference between past and present ways of understanding a work' in terms of literary and historical contexts, and which 'thereby challenges as platonizing dogma the apparently self-evident dictum of philological metaphysics that literature is timelessly present and that it has objective meaning, determined once and for all and directly open to the interpreter at any time' (23). Truth to life, for instance, is not a universal criterion of greatness in literature, but a value which characterizes the period of humanism, seen as historically determinate, distinct from both the middle ages and the modern period, when the mimetic theory is without authority (26).

Jauss, however, is concerned primarily with literary history, with the analysis of the process by which the new and challenging becomes familiar and effortless. For a theory of the reading process itself we need to turn to Wolfgang Iser, probably the leading exponent of the Aesthetics of Reception. Iser is fully aware of the theoretical problems involved in discussing 'the reader' as authority for a single mode of reading. Empirical readers, whose responses are documented, impose one kind of limitation on the possibilities of interpretation, and hypothetical readers, whether ideal figures or contemporaries of the author, inevitably impose others, different in each case. He himself settles for the concept of the 'implied reader', a figure who is constructed by the text in the sense that 'he embodies all those predispositions necessary for a literary work to exercise its effect – predispositions laid down, not by an empirical outside reality, but by the text itself (Iser 1978: 34). There follows an extremely instructive account of the process by which the reader produces a meaning which is neither wholly determined – because of the 'indeterminacies' created by the juxtaposition of 'perspectives' in the text – nor entirely subjective – because the formal properties of the text construct a role for the reader. Readings, therefore, are neither given nor arbitrary.

Once again, however, Iser's theory suppresses the relationship between language and experience. He argues that the words of the text stimulate 'mental images' which are the 'basic feature of ideation' (135 ff). The text is thus 'translated' into the reader's consciousness, where it becomes part of his or her personal experience. Reading is an educative process in which the reader assimilates unfamiliar experience, or lives for a time an alien life (155–6). Thus, the basic model is the familiar concept of communication between individual subjects. Recognizing the theoretical problems both of the expressive theory and of the concept of a single model reader, Iser replaces the empirical author and the ideal reader with an implied author and an implied reader, and he probably arrives at as sophisticated an analysis of the relationship between them as the communication model allows.

Iser's *The Act of Reading* is in many ways an excellent theoretical account of what, in all their variety, most liberal humanist readers in the second half of the twentieth century probably actually *do* when they read. But as Iser's very conventional specific readings demonstrate, it is no more than that.

A more radical break with the values of expressive realism was offered by Stanley Fish, whose 'interpretive communities' have entered the critical vocabulary. Fish's discussion of 'the reader in *Paradise Lost*' caused considerable excitement when *Surprised by Sin* first appeared in 1967. This was followed by the equally widely discussed *Self-Consuming Artifacts* in 1972, subtitled 'the experience of seventeenth-century literature'. The reader's experience was fundamental to Fish's approach. Reading, he argued there, was an activity, a process, and meanings were events in the reader's consciousness. The reader thus replaced the author as the origin of the meaning of the text.

Fish's *Is There a Text in This Class?* was published in 1980. The new project was to account for the fact that, while meanings were to be found in readers' heads, and might thus be expected to be purely individual, there was in practice a high degree of critical consensus about the meanings of specific texts. The reason for this, it appeared, was that readers belong to interpretive communities, in the sense that they share assumptions and expectations about both the reading process and texts themselves. We interpret as we do because that is how our community interprets. Our capacity to make sense of a specific text is constrained by the practices of the interpretive community we participate in.

Do we, then, all read the same text in identical ways? Not at all, Fish acknowledges. Other readings are the products of other interpretive communities. If we are not happy with the constraints a group imposes, not at home in that practice of reading, we are free to join another. Indeed, we are already by definition members of another, since there is no interpretation in isolation from culturally imposed assumptions and expectations, no direct and solitary encounter with 'the text itself'.

The welcome inclusion of culture in Fish's account of the reading process led, however, to a problem of a different kind, and in 1989 in *Doing What Comes Naturally* Fish addressed the question, among others, of change. If readers learn to read from their communities, and accept the constraints involved, how do they ever come to change their minds? The answer, it seemed, was that interpretive communities are large; they embrace variety. His own, for instance, includes the constraint that it is incumbent on readers, confronted by a proposition formulated authoritatively, to engage with it rationally and not to reject it without good reason. Moreover, his own also positively encourages its members to read about other disciplines, and in doing so, they may learn more about how to practise their own differently. The outside influence that promoted change was thus already, in a sense, inside the community (141–60).

Fish's position is eminently plausible and, with the support of his breezy stylistic insouciance and no-nonsense manner, it has made many converts. But there is a theoretical difficulty here, as with all idealist accounts of the reading process. If, as Fish insists, 'meaning cannot be . . . derived from the shape of marks on a page' (1989: 4), if meaning is no more than an *idea* in the head of the reader, how do we know what we are reading? Or what, in other words, is our reading an interpretation of? If the text itself exerts no determinations, as Fish insists, how can I tell whether the text I make sense of is *Paradise Lost* or *The Pickwick Papers*? Presumably this distinction is also no more than conventional. There seems no other reason why my interpretation of one, determined by my interpretive community, should differ perceptibly from my reading of the other. But, you will surely answer, the facts are different; the plot and characters, for example, are not the same. And I should have to reply by asking how, according to the theory, you know that.

Let us be clear. Fish is not making the modest claim that the interpetive community exerts an influence; he is not suggesting that reading establishes a relationship between a culturally constructed reader and a text. Here is his own appeal to his readers, written archly in the third person, to engage with the case he makes:

> we could even attend to Stanley Fish when he argues in *Is There a Text in This Class?* and elsewhere that we cannot check our interpretive accounts against the facts of the text because it is only within our accounts – that is, within an already assumed set of stipulative definitions and evidentiary criteria – that the text and its facts, or, rather, *a* text and its facts, emerge and become available for inspection.
>
> (Fish 1989: 143–4)

The 'facts of the text' are already incorporated into our accounts of it, and these are determined by our interpretive community.

How then, the same essay asks, can we be sure that *Paradise Lost* goes on existing as an object when our accounts of it change, that it continues to be *Paradise Lost* and not something else? Is this too purely a matter of convention? Apparently not. And here the writing begins to bluster, as the argument comes up against its own conceptual difficulties:

> The fact that the objects we have are all objects that appear to us in the context of some practice, of work done by some interpretive community, doesn't mean that they are not objects or that we don't have them or that they exert no pressure on us.
>
> (153)

The text not only exists, then, as an object, but exerts pressures on us. As far as I can see, either these pressures are pressures on our interpretation, in which case the text plays a part in the construction of its meaning, or they are not, in which case the pressures exerted remain mysterious and undefined, and the assertion evades its own necessary contradiction of what has gone before.

On the first reading, Fish's view represents a moderate advance on expressive realism, to the degree that it challenges the belief that meaning inheres timelessly in the text as an expression of the author's ideas. On the second, idealism recognizes the limits on rational argument imposed by its own denial of the material role of the text in the reading process.

In practice, reading is a transaction, a relation between the cultural vocabulary of the text and the cultural vocabulary of the reader. The transfer of meaning from its place in the mind of the author to a similar place in the mind of a culturally determined reader, denying the role of language in the constitution of meaning, does not solve the problems it was designed to counter.

To liberate new ways of reading which overcome the theoretical problems and the practical limitations I have discussed in this necessarily selective account of some of the available theories, we need a new theoretical framework which makes a fundamental break with the propositions of common sense. The assaults on expressive realism I have sketched do not constitute such a break. Post-Saussurean linguistics, however, undermines common sense in a more radical way and so provides a theoretical framework which permits the development of a genuinely radical critical practice.

3

CRITICISM AND MEANING

POST-SAUSSUREAN LINGUISTICS

The failure of each of these theoretical assaults on expressive realism to break with the commonsense view of language meant that while each in turn had a fashionable following, and while New Criticism even came to prevail as an orthodoxy, particularly in the United States, common sense has continued to flourish and expressive realism, with only minor concessions to its opponents, survived largely unscathed. The New Critics, Northrop Frye and the reader-theorists stayed within the empiricist-idealist problematic, and in doing so they permitted an easy eclecticism, a critical practice which appropriated and reconciled elements from some or all of them, without being compelled to confront the implications of its own assumptions and presuppositions.

The logical possibility of expressive realism, however, is put in question by post-Saussurean linguistics, which challenges empiricist-idealist ways of understanding the relationship between language and the world. I use the term 'post-Saussurean' not simply in a chronological sense, but to identify work which traces a direct descent from the radical elements in Saussure's theory of the sign, so that Chomsky's transformational generative grammar, for instance, is not post-Saussurean in this sense, whatever Chomsky's importance for work in linguistics as a whole. Saussure's *Course in General Linguistics*, published in 1916, has exerted a profound influence not only on linguistics itself but on the rise of semiology (or semiotics), the science of signs which Saussure postulated in a tantalizing passage of the *Course* (Saussure 1974: 16). The full implications of Saussure's work, both for language and for the other signifying systems of society, are still in the process of being recognized. The study of literature as a signifying practice is currently being transformed by an increasing realization of Saussure's importance.

The most revolutionary element in Saussure's position was his insistence that language is not a nomenclature, a way of naming things which already exist, but a system of differences with no positive terms. He argued that, far from providing a set of labels for entities which exist independently in the world, language precedes the existence of independent entities, making the world intelligible by differentiating between concepts. This hypothesis requires amplification and justification.

In Saussure's theory, language is a system of signs. A sign consists of a signifier (the sound-image or the written shape) and a signified (a concept). The sound-image *dog* is inseparably linked in English with the concept *dog*, and the two can be isolated from each other only analytically. 'Language can . . . be compared with a sheet of paper: thought is the front and the sound the back; one cannot cut the front without cutting the back at the same time; likewise in language, one can neither divide sounds from thought nor thought from sound' (Saussure 1974: 113).

The inseparability of the signifier and the signified, the fact that for a speaker of English the sound-image *dog* belongs with the concept *dog* and not, say, with the concept *cow*, creates the illusion of the transparency of language. 'It is in the nature of language to be overlooked' (Hjelmslev 1969: 5). We feel as if *dog* is a label for something which exists unproblematically, in some ultimate and incontestable way, and it is only by an effort of thought that it is possible to challenge this feeling. Saussure challenged it. He was not the first to do so — the problem is the central (and unresolved) issue in Plato's *Cratylus* — but his work exerted a powerful influence on subsequent linguistic theory.

Saussure's argument depends on the different division of the chain of meaning in different languages. 'If words stood for pre-existing concepts, they would all have exact equivalents in meaning from one language to the next; but this is not true' (Saussure 1974: 116). The truth is that different languages divide or articulate the world in different ways. Saussure gives a number of examples. For instance, where French has the single word *mouton*, English differentiates between *mutton*, which we eat, and *sheep*, which roams the hills. Jonathan Culler cites the distinction between *river* and *stream* in English in contrast to *fleuve* and *rivière* in French. In English what distinguishes a river from a stream is size; in French a *fleuve* flows into the sea, a *rivière* into another *rivière* or a *fleuve* (Culler 1976: 24). Some languages divide the spectrum differently from others. In Welsh the colour *glas* (blue), like the Latin *glaucus*, includes elements which English would identify as green or grey. The boundaries are placed differently in the two languages and the Welsh equivalent of English *grey* might be *glas* or *llwyd* (brown):

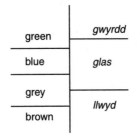

(Hjelmslev 1969: 53)

In other words, colour terms, like language itself, form a system of differences, readily experienced as natural, given, but in practice constructed by the language itself.

Nor is this process of differentiation confined to objects of the senses. The distinction in French between *science* and *connaissance* does not correspond to the English *science* and *knowledge*: indeed each term can be translated from one to the other only approximately and by what seems a very circumlocutory process, because the words have the effect of limiting each other's range of meaning within the interdependent whole which constitutes each language. Signs are defined by their difference from each other in the network of signs which is the signifying system. Languages which have a past historic tense have a corresponding restriction on the use of the simple past. In proto-Germanic there is no future tense, and in consequence the value of the present tense is different from its value in languages which have both tenses (Saussure 1974: 117). These non-correspondences, often experienced as difficult to grasp in the process of learning a new language, have far-reaching theoretical implications. We are compelled to argue either that our own language has got its concepts 'right' in some absolute way, and that all the others are to varying degrees out of step, or that concepts are purely differential, and that they are determined not by their positive content but by their relations with the other terms of the system. 'Signs function, then, not through their intrinsic value but through their relative position' (118).

We use signifiers to mark off areas of a continuum. The spectrum again illustrates the point. It is not that I cannot distinguish between shades of blue but that the language insists on a difference, which readily comes to seem fundamental, *natural*, between blue and green. The world, which without signification would be experienced as a continuum, is divided up by language into entities which then readily come to be experienced as essentially distinct. The way in which we use signifiers to create differences appears in the labelling of otherwise identical toothmugs, 'his' and 'hers'. Jacques Lacan illustrates the point with the following diagram:

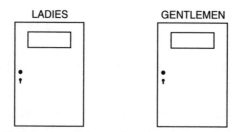

Here the signifiers, *Ladies* and *Gentlemen*, are used to create a distinction. The image of the twin doors symbolises 'through the solitary confinement offered Western Man for the satisfaction of his natural needs away from home, the imperative that he seems to share with the great majority of primitive communities by which his public life is subjected to the laws of urinary segregation' (Lacan 1977a: 151).

The quotation from Lacan draws attention to another important element of Saussure's general thesis: language is a social fact. Only a social group can generate signs. Noises which have no meaning may be purely individual, but meaning, intelligibility, cannot by definition be produced in isolation. The sign is in an important sense arbitrary – the sound *dog* has no more necessary or natural connection with the concept *dog* than has *chien* or *Hund*. Even onomatopeic words, which seem to imitate the sounds they signify, are by no means international: French dogs say *ouaoua*; *to splash* in French is *éclabousser*. And it is the arbitrariness of the sign which points to the fact that language is a matter of convention. The linguistic community 'agrees' to attach a specific signified to a specific signifier, though in reality, of course, its agreement is not explicitly sought but merely manifested in the fact that certain linguistic units are used and understood. 'The arbitrary nature of the sign explains in turn why the social fact alone can create a linguistic system. The community is necessary if values that owe their existence solely to usage and general acceptance are to be set up' (Saussure 1974: 113). And conversely, of course, a community needs a signifying system: social organization and social exchange, the ordering of the processes of producing the means of subsistence, is impossible without the existence of a signification. Language therefore comes into being at the same time as society.

This suggests that while the individual sign is arbitrary there is an important sense in which the signifying system as a whole is not. Meaning is public and conventional, the result not of individual intention but of inter-individual intelligibility. In other words, meaning is socially constructed, and the social construction of the signifying system is intimately related, therefore, to the social formation itself. On the basis of Saussure's work it is possible to argue that, in so far as language is a way of articulating experience, it necessarily participates in *ideology*, the sum of the ways in which people both live and represent to themselves their relationship to the conditions of their existence. Ideology is *inscribed in signifying practices* – in discourses, myths, presentations and re-presentations of the way 'things' 'are' – and to this extent it is inscribed in the language. I shall discuss ideology in more detail in Chapter 4. For the moment let me suggest that, while ideology cannot be reduced to language and, more important, language certainly cannot be reduced to ideology, the signifying system can have an important role in naturalizing the way things are. Because it is characteristic of language to be overlooked, the differences it constructs may seem to be natural, universal and unalterable, when in practice they may be produced by a specific form of social organization.

The women's movement, to take a commonplace instance, has drawn attention to the inscription in signifying practice of the patriarchal organization of society. One example is the use of *man, men* to mean *people* in expressions like 'Western Man', 'men produce their means of subsistence'. The words for male persons are also used as the common gender nouns in these instances and this has the effect of constituting an implicit equation between *people* and *male people*, so that women come to be represented in discourse as a secondary sex, differentiated from an implied male norm. That *he* subsumes *she* in legal documents and in generalizations ('if an employee has a grievance, he will report it . . .'; 'the reader will make up his mind') has similar implications, and it is no accident that in a period when women are becoming increasingly conscious of the effects of patriarchy, they are challenging these linguistic usages, insisting on *people, he or she, his or her*.

The way in which ideology is inscribed in ordinary language is also apparent in the differentiation between women who are available for marriage and those who are not (*Miss, Mrs*). The marking of this difference implies a distinction which is in some way essential between married and unmarried women, while men remain Mr whether they are married or not. The usefulness of making and publicly labelling the distinction between married and unmarried women in a society in which men have been conventionally responsible for taking the initiative in selecting a marriage partner is easily overlooked in favour of its naturalness. The introduction of *Ms* has ideological implications, as well as the advantage of saving time or embarrassment in addressing women whose marital status is not known.

We are aware of the connection between language and ideology in these instances because the position of women in the social structure and in ideology is currently in transition, and here the changes which are taking place are predominantly radical changes. In a quite different area, however, it may be that the recent and increasingly common blurring of the distinction between *uninterested* and *disinterested* is also ideologically significant. It could be argued that as capitalism increasingly equates wealth with happiness (while also contradictorily asserting, of course, that the best things in life are free), *interest* as intellectual curiosity or concern is gradually ceasing to seem distinct from *interest* as material or economic concern, so that *disinterested* (detached, having nothing to gain) is becoming synonymous with *uninterested* (bored).

A historical instance of the relationship between social formation, ideology and language may make the point more persuasively. The medieval usage *gentil* has no precise modern equivalent. The concept inscribed in the word (aristocratic, courteous, virtuous) is not fully signified by its descendants, *gentle* and *genteel*, and the use of these words with the full meaning of *gentil* becomes increasingly rare from the Renaissance onwards. Meanwhile, *nice*, which during the course of its history has meant a number of things including *lazy, foolish* and *lascivious*, took on its predominant modern meaning of *agreeable* in the late eighteenth century (O.E.D., 15), the period of the rise of industrial capitalism, when the bourgeoisie became firmly installed as the ruling class. A *nice* person is a 'democratic' concept in a way that a *gentil* person is not. *Nice* has no aristocratic connotations, but it makes concessions to the middle-class proprieties in certain contexts ('nice manners', 'nicely brought up'). Clearly here the decline of *gentil* and the rise of *nice* are not arbitrary but are related to changes in the social formation: broadly, *gentil* is feudal, *nice* bourgeois-democratic.

If signifieds are not pre-existing, given concepts, but changeable and contingent concepts, and if changes in signifying practice are related to changes in the social formation, the notion of language as a neutral nomenclature functioning as an instrument of communication of meanings which exist independently of it is clearly untenable. Language is a system which pre-exists the individual and in which the individual produces meaning. In learning its native language the child learns a set of differentiating concepts which identify not *given entities* but *socially constructed meanings*. Language in an important sense speaks us. This does not mean that all discourse is trapped in linguistic determinism. Language is infinitely productive (Hjelmslev 1969: 109–10) and it is in language that the ideology inscribed in the language can be challenged. But it does mean that an organization of the world which seems natural is not necessarily so. Differences and distinctions which seem obvious, a matter of common sense, cannot be taken for granted, since common sense itself is to a large degree a linguistic construct. Roland Barthes's *Mythologies*, originally published in 1957, has come to be regarded as the classic exposition of the ways in which ideological myths are naturalized to form common sense in our society.

The difficulty of challenging common sense, however, becomes apparent in the context of the close relationship between language and thinking. Language is not, of course, the only signifying system. Images, gestures, social behaviour, clothes are all socially invested with meaning, are all elements of the symbolic order: language is simply the most flexible and perhaps the most complex of the signifying systems. Thought, if not exclusively dependent on language, is inconceivable without the symbolic order in general. 'Thought is nothing other than the power to construct representations of things and to operate on these representations. It is in essence symbolic' (Benveniste 1971: 25). As a result, mental categories and the laws of thought tend to reproduce the system of differences inscribed in the symbolic order. 'The varieties of philosophical or spiritual experience depend unconsciously on a classification which language brings about only for the reason that it is language and that it is symbolic' (Benveniste 1971: 6). There is no unmediated experience of the world; knowledge is possible only in terms of the categories and the laws of the symbolic order. Far from expressing a unique perception of the world, authors produce meaning out of the available system of differences, and texts are intelligible in so far as they participate in it.

Again it is important to stress that this is not an argument for determinism. We are not enslaved by the conventions which prevail in our own time. Authors do not inevitably simply reiterate the timeworn patterns of signification. Analysis reveals that at any given moment the categories and laws of the symbolic order are full of contradictions, ambiguities and inconsistencies which function as a source of possible change. The role of ideology is to suppress these contradictions in the interests of the preservation of the existing social formation, but their presence ensures that it is always possible, with whatever difficulty, to identify them, to recognize ideology for what it is, and to take an active part in transforming it by producing new meanings. The relationship between language and thought explains, however, the tenacity of the empiricist-idealist theory of language. Language is *experienced* as a nomenclature because its existence precedes our 'understanding' of the world. Words seem to be symbols for things because things are inconceivable outside the system of differences which constitutes the language. Similarly, these very things seem to be represented in the mind, in an autonomous realm of thought, because thought is in essence symbolic, dependent on the differences brought about by the symbolic order. And so language is 'overlooked', suppressed in favour of a quest for meaning in experience and/or in the mind. The world of things and subjectivity then become the twin guarantors of truth.

The relationship between language and thought also explains the intensity of the resistance to new meanings and new ways of analysing the world, just as it explains the difficulty of unfamiliar concepts (signifieds) which cannot come into existence without new and unfamiliar discourses – new signifiers and relations between signifiers. To challenge common sense is to challenge the inscription of common sense in language.

From this post-Saussurean perspective it is clear that the theory of literature as expressive realism is no longer tenable. The claim that a literary form reflects the world is simply tautological. If by 'the world' we understand the world we experience, the world differentiated by language, then the claim that realism reflects the world means that realism reflects the world constructed in language. This is a tautology. If texts link concepts through a system of signs which signify by means of their relationship to each other rather than to entities in the world, and if literature is a signifying practice, all it can reflect is the order inscribed in particular discourses, not the nature of the world. Thus, what is intelligible as realism is the conventional and therefore familiar, 'recognizable' articulation and distribution of concepts. It is intelligible as 'realistic' precisely because it reproduces what we already seem to know.

Equally, the subjectivity of a specially perceptive author is no guarantee of the authority of a specific perception of the world. If thought is not independent of the differences inscribed in language, then subjectivity itself is inconceivable outside language. I shall discuss this more fully in Chapter 4.

THE CONSTRUCTION OF MEANING

Realism is plausible not because it reflects the world, but because it is constructed out of what is (discursively) familiar. The process of constructing meaning by reproducing what is familiar can be illustrated briefly and clearly by reference to a non-literary signifying system, advertising. (In what follows I owe a good deal to the very interesting analysis provided in Judith Williamson's book, *Decoding Advertisements*.) If, for example, we consider half a dozen advertisements for different perfumes, we see the Saussurean system of differences literally in the process of construction. Perfumes differ chemically from each other, of course: they smell different. But their promotion depends on the association of a smell with a social 'meaning'. Through the juxtaposition of 'semes' (signifieds of connotation) the product comes to be intelligible as the signifier of a cultural and ideological signified,[1] and to the extent that the construction of the process of signification is overlooked and the naming, packaging and advertising are seen as transparent, the product becomes the signifier of specific cultural and ideological values. It is the role of publicity to *characterize* perfumes, to differentiate them from each other in ideological (as opposed to merely physical) terms, to create distinct social signifieds for them, to give them meaning.

The six advertisements I have chosen more or less at random from issues of women's magazines demonstrate how the process of characterization is achieved. Each advertisement shows a 'realistic' photograph of a different type of woman. To enable us to identify each type certain familiar cultural codes are invoked, and we are invited to make an association between their meanings and the product. What is important is that the codes are already part of our knowledge.

The *Chique* advertisement shows a woman in a large hat, a silk shirt and the jacket of a suit. The top half of her face is invisible, shaded by the brim of her hat. We 'read' this as sophisticated, mysterious, classically elegant, and to do so we draw on the current photographic codes, in which the fact that the woman's eyes are hidden connotes mystery, and on the code of dress which is not, of course, confined to pictorial modes of representation, but which is commonly invoked as a means of characterization in fiction of all kinds. A different kind of sophistication is signified in the advertisement for Yves Saint Laurent's *Rive Gauche*. Here the French name is supported by a caption in (not very difficult) French, which enables the reader to *experience* a feeling of sophistication in being able to understand it. The model is wearing brightly coloured, highly fashionable clothes, and stares coolly and provocatively back at the spectator. The *Estivalia* advertisement shows a woman in a long white dress gazing off to the left. Soft focus photography and the absence of bright lighting connote twilight and romance. The setting is organic, perhaps a walled garden. Behind the model and to the right is a barely identified figure, quite out of focus. The caption reads, 'for daydream believers'. Here we are invited to construct a miniature narrative, a 'daydream' story which takes account of the mysterious figure, the woman and the setting, to perform the daydreaming endorsed by the advertisement. It would be easy to do so on the basis of countless romantic films, stories and novels, and by doing so we should be participating actively in the process of constructing the 'meaning' of Estivalia. The impression is that we create an individual daydream out of our own subjectivity: in practice the range of probable narratives is constrained by the particular semes juxtaposed in the photograph. The components of the image – shadowy figure, white dress, evening, tree – tend to propel us in a very specific direction. The picture is not particularly rich in plurality, at least for members of our society.

These three advertisements draw on the cultural stereotypes of femininity, and in 'reading' them with such ease we demonstrate the familiarity of these stereotypes. The remaining three advertisements present 'liberated' women, now also rapidly becoming recuperated for ideology as a new set of stereotypes. These figures are in reality no less 'feminine', no less offered as objects for the male gaze. *Blasé* shows a woman in a shirt and trousers, a sweater tied round her neck, walking towards the camera with windswept hair. *Charlie* is a woman in trousers with a document case, striding purposefully across the tarmac of an international airport. *Charivari* shows a woman in trousers and a flat cap balancing exuberantly on a bicycle in a cobbled street. Again we construct connections between their clothes, their settings and their actions, unconsciously – or at least without conscious effort – producing a signified which is in practice predetermined by the familiarity of the signifiers.

These advertisements are a source of information about ideology, about semiotics, about the cultural and photographic codes of our society, and to that extent – and only to that extent – they tell us about the world. And yet they possess all the technical properties of realism. Literary realism works in very much the same kind of way. Like the advertisements, it constructs its signifieds out of juxtapositions of signifiers which are intelligible not as direct reflections of an unmediated reality but because we are familiar with the signifying systems from which they are drawn, linguistic, literary, semiotic. This process is apparent in, for instance, the construction of character in the novel.

Here a brief demonstration of the process is less easy than it is in the case of advertisements, since the character signifiers of, say, the central figure are usually distributed throughout the text. None the less fictional characterization, though often more complex than the characterization of the perfumes, is a process of construction from an assembly of semes in exactly the same way. George Eliot's *Middlemarch*, for example, presents a subtle and detailed analysis of Dorothea Brooke in a way that has encouraged generations of readers to feel that she has a life beyond the pages of the novel. Criticism has conventionally recognized in Dorothea a 'rounded character' whose vitality is palpable and whose inner nature accounts for her actions. But of course Dorothea is as patently constructed out of the signifying systems as the photographs which characterize *Chique* or *Estivalia*. The juxtaposition of the signifiers is more complex, more inclined to be contradictory; the signifiers themselves are in some cases more esoteric; but the fundamental process of construction is very similar. Consider, for instance, the opening sentences of *Middlemarch*. They constitute only the beginning of the construction process, but they will be linked to a network of semes distributed throughout the novel, with the effect of creating an impression of a character of complexity and depth.

Miss Brooke had that kind of beauty which seems to be thrown into relief by poor dress. Her hand and wrist were so finely formed that she could wear sleeves not less bare of style than those in which the Blessed Virgin appeared to Italian painters; and her profile as well as her stature and bearing seemed to gain the more dignity from her plain garments, which by the side of provincial fashion gave her the impressiveness of a fine quotation from the Bible, – or from one of our elder poets, – in a paragraph of today's newspaper.

Here the opening sentence employs what Barthes identifies as the 'code of reference' (1975: 18), an allusion to a shared body of knowledge, 'that kind of beauty which [as we all recognize] seems to be thrown into relief by poor dress'. The phrase lends the authority of an apparent familiarity to the image constructed from the genuinely familiar semes which follow and which attribute to Dorothea (with whatever trace of irony) qualities of fineness, austerity, purity, otherworldliness, timeless worth, rarity. Subsequent passages deepen the image, constructing less favourably received but equally readily intelligible meanings: fervour, impetuousness, pride. In consequence Dorothea lives.

This necessary familiarity does not mean that realism can never surprise us. Of course it can do so through unexpected juxtapositions and complexities. But it assembles these juxtapositions and complexities out of what we already know, and it is for this reason that we experience it as realistic. To this extent it is a predominantly conservative form. The experience of reading a realist text is ultimately reassuring, however harrowing the events of the story, because the world evoked in the fiction, its patterns of cause and effect, of social relationships and moral values, largely confirm the patterns of the world we seem to know.

Realism is a culturally relative concept, of course, and many avant-garde movements have successively introduced formal changes in the name of increased verisimilitude. But the term is useful in distinguishing between those forms which tend to efface their own textuality, their existence as discourse, and those which explicitly draw attention to it. Realism offers itself as transparent. The rejection of the concept of a literary form which reflects the world, however, has led some post-Saussurean critical theorists to use the phrase 'classic realism' to designate literature which creates an effect or illusion of reality.

This is not just another gratuitous piece of jargon. 'Classic realism' makes it possible to unite categories which have been divided by the empiricist assumption that the text reflects the world. By implying Saussurean quotation marks round 'realism', the phrase permits the inclusion of all those fictional forms which create the illusion while we read that what is narrated is 'really' and intelligibly happening: *The Hobbit* and *The Rainbow*, *The War of the Worlds* and *Middlemarch*. Speaking animals, elves, or Martians are no impediment to intelligibility and credibility if they conform to patterns of speech and behaviour consistent with a 'recognizable' system. Even in fantasy events, however improbable in themselves, are *related* to each other in familiar ways. The plausibility of the individual signifieds is far less important to the reading process than the familiarity of the connections between the signifiers. It is the set of relationships between characters or events, or between characters and events, which makes fantasy convincing.

THE PLURALITY OF MEANING

If post-Saussurean linguistics undermines the possibility of expressive realism, it is equally apparent that it puts in question the theoretical positions from which I have argued that expressive realism has been attacked. Any attempt to locate a guarantee of meaning in concepts of human experience or human hopes and fears, which are outside history and outside textuality, is as inadequate as the formalist belief that the guarantee of meaning is eternally inscribed in the language of the text itself. The critical assaults on expressive realism sketched in Chapter 2 all constitute, whether consciously or unconciously, quests for a theory of meaning. The object in each case is to locate a guarantee of the meaning of the text. Expressive realism finds this guarantee in the author's mind, or in the world we all know, or in the conjunction of the two – the author's perception of the world we know. New Critism is uncertain whether to locate it in language or in human experience. Frye finds it in human anxieties and aspirations. The reader-theorists finally invoke a reader, variously defined, whose responses constitute the authority for the meaning of the text.

The problem confronted (or evaded) by all these theories can be quite simply demonstrated. To take an extreme and fairly obvious example, if I encounter the sentence, 'democracy will ensure that we extend the boundaries of civilization', it is apparent that there are several ways in which I might understand it. Possibly 'democracy' would evoke free speech, consumer choice and parliamentary elections; 'civilization' would suggest the antithesis of barbarism; and its extension would seem a product of the preservation of democratic values in a world where totalitarianism constantly threatens. Alternatively, however, I might understand 'democracy' to be a more radical seizure of power by the people, so that 'civilization', a way of life hitherto the prerogative of a privileged few, would become accessible to everyone. Or I might read the sentence entirely ironically to mean that the introduction of consumer choice ('a hollow sham') into the third world will ensure that by developing capitalism there we impose our own ('decadent') cultural and political values. Other interpretations could almost certainly be produced, and these various readings have nothing to do with whether I agree with the statement or not (except in so far as my agreement would probably be conditional on my interpretation). On the contrary, they depend on the connotative meanings of the words themselves.

But what does the sentence 'really' mean? If I invoke a specific *speaker* – a Conservative M.P., a committed socialist or the Vice-President of Coca Cola – I can readily attribute to the sentence a single meaning guaranteed by what I take to be the intentions of the speaker. Alternatively, if I posit a specific *hearer*, reader of the *Daily Telegraph*, social democrat or South American guerrilla, I can locate a single interpretation. Neither is very satisfactory: both speaker and hearer are to some degree conjectural, the product of speculation and generalization. But these practices constitute the respective bases of the expressive theory and reader-theory. The alternative has been to find an authority for meaning in the world we experience (New Criticism) or the world we aspire to (Northrop Frye).

What is apparent from the example of the sentence about democracy and civilization is the extent to which language is a social fact. The meanings of the sentence vary from one political analysis to another (conservative, socialist, liberationist, etc.), and to the extent that the hearer participates in these political word pictures, he or she finds in the sentence one or more of the possible readings. In other words, the meaning of this sentence is *plural*. But this is emphatically not to say that it is subjective. In reality we all participate in a range of knowledges – political, literary, scientific and so on – and these are 'subjective' only to the extent that they – and the contradictions and collisions between them – construct our world of meaning and experience. A word or a sentence is intelligible only within a specific discourse, and discourse is in turn constitutive of subjectivity, as I shall argue in Chapter 4. To posit the subject as an authority for a single meaning is to ignore the degree to which subjectivity itself is a discursive construct. To find a guarantee of meaning in the world or in experience is to ignore the fact that our experience of the world is itself constituted in language.

Of course, the example I have given is an artificial one. 'Democracy' notoriously means all things to all speakers, and in any case we do not normally come across such sentences in isolation. The context of the sentence might be expected to narrow the range of possible readings. On the other hand, the possibility of finding plurality in a succession of sentences might well be greater still. Its context in the work as a whole may seem to indicate that certain readings are not appropriate to an individual sentence, but this context, itself made up of sentences (or elements from other semiotic systems), is also subject to interpretation, and in narrowing some kinds of plurality, context may open others. And in any case, literature, dealing in the great (discursive) ambiguities of love and death, sacrifice and revenge, and traditionally believed to be rich in connotation and elusive in its nuances, is surely all the more susceptible of a plurality of interpretations than a crude and commonplace political slogan.

A NEW CRITICAL PRACTICE

It is the recurrent suppression of the role of language which has limited this plurality, and this suppression is in turn ideological. The task of a new critical practice is first to identify the effects of the limitation which confines 'correct' reading to an acceptance of the position from which the text is most 'obviously' intelligible, the position of a transcendent subject addressed by an autonomous and authoritative author. Thereafter it becomes possible to refuse this limitation, to liberate the plurality of the text, to reject the 'obvious' and to produce meaning.

The theory which defines and delimits the new critical practice brings together specific elements of separate theoretical knowledges, even though these knowledges, produced to serve distinct theoretical and practical ends, are not in their entirety compatible with each other. It is my hypothesis, for instance, that both Althusserian Marxism and

Lacanian psychoanalysis may contribute to an understanding of the role of literature and the possibilities for literary criticism, although, as they stand, they are far from fully consistent with each other. Neither of these theories in isolation seems to me to be able to offer an adequate account of the work of literature. Very briefly, Lacan apparently leaves little room for history, while Althusser's theory of subjectivity leaves little room for change. I have therefore drawn on each position without dwelling on the incompatibilities between them. To justify this procedure in theoretical terms would necessitate a very different kind of book, using the work of Rosalind Coward and John Ellis, perhaps, in *Language and Materialism*, and invoking in addition a theory of culture which would permit us to identify the historical specificity of modes of subjectivity. In the mean time my present procedure seems to me to be admissible if it generates a productive critical practice.

4

ADDRESSING THE SUBJECT

IDEOLOGY

Without assuming that a text independently generates a determinate, transhistorical and universally recognizable reading, it can, of course, be argued not only that an intimate relationship exists between ideology and specific reading practices, but also that these reading practices are fostered by some texts rather than others. In his influential essay on 'Ideology and Ideological State Apparatuses', Louis Althusser includes literature among the ideological apparatuses which contribute to the process of *reproducing* the *relations of production*, the social relationships which are the necessary condition for the existence and perpetuation of the capitalist mode of production (1971: 121–73).[1]

He does not here develop the argument concerning literature but, in the context of his own concept of ideology, and also of the work of Roland Barthes on literature and Jacques Lacan on psychoanalysis, it is possible to construct an account of some of the implications for critical theory and practice of Althusser's position. The argument is not only that literature re-presents the myths and imaginary versions of real social relationships which constitute ideology, but also that classic realist fiction, the dominant literary form of the nineteenth century and arguably of the twentieth, 'interpellates' the reader, addresses itself to him or her directly, offering the reader as the place from which the text is most 'obviously' intelligible, the position of the *subject in (and of) ideology*.

According to Althusser's reading (rereading) of Marx, ideology is not simply a set of illusions, as *The German Ideology* might appear to argue, but a range of representations (images, stories, myths) concerning the real relations in which people live.[2] But what is represented in ideology is 'not the system of the real relations which govern the existence of individuals, but the imaginary relation of those individuals to the real relations in which they live' (Althusser 1971: 155). In other words, ideology is both a real and an imaginary relation to the world – real in that it is the way that people really live their relationship to the social relations which govern their existence, but imaginary in that it discourages a full understanding of these conditions of existence and the ways in which people are socially constituted within them. It is not, therefore, to be thought of as a system of ideas in people's heads, nor as the expression at a higher level of real material relationships, but as the necessary condition of action within the social formation. Althusser talks of ideology as a 'material practice' in this sense: it exists in the behaviour of people acting according to their beliefs (155–9).

As the necessary condition of action, ideology resides in commonplaces and truisms, as well as in philosophical and religious systems. It is apparent in all that is 'obvious' to us, in 'obviousnesses, which we cannot fail to recognize and before which we have the inevitable and natural reaction of crying out (aloud or in the "still, small voice of conscience"): "That's obvious! That's right! That's true!"' (161). If it is true, however, it is not the whole truth. Ideology obscures the real conditions of existence by presenting partial truths. It is a set of omissions, gaps rather than lies, smoothing over contradictions, appearing to provide answers to questions which in practice it evades, and masquerading as coherence in the interests of the social relations generated by and necessary to the reproduction of the existing mode of production.

It is important to stress, of course, that ideology is by no means a set of deliberate distortions foisted upon a helpless populace by a corrupt and cynical bourgeoisie. If there are sinister groups of men in shirt-sleeves purveying illusions to the public, these are not the real makers of ideology. In that sense, it has no creators. But, according to

Althusser, ideological practices are supported and reproduced in the institutions of our society which he calls Ideological State Apparatuses (ISAs). Unlike the Repressive State Apparatus, which works by force (the police, the penal system and the army), the ISAs persuade us to consent to the existing mode of production.

The central ISA in contemporary capitalism is the educational system, which prepares children to act in accordance with the values of society, by inculcating in them the dominant versions of appropriate behaviour, as well as history, social studies and, of course, literature. Among the allies of the educational ISA are the family, the law, the media and the arts, each helping to represent and reproduce the myths and beliefs necessary to induce people to work within the existing social formation.

THE SUBJECT

The destination of all ideology is the *subject*. The subject is what speaks, or signifies, and it is the role of ideology to *construct people as subjects*:

> I say: the category of the subject is constitutive of all ideology, but at the same time and immediately I add that *the category of the subject is only constitutive of all ideology insofar as all ideology has the function (which defines it) of 'constituting' concrete individuals as subjects*.

> (Althusser 1971: 160)

Within bourgeois ideology it appears 'obvious' that people are autonomous individuals, possessed of a subjectivity that is the source of their beliefs and actions. That people are unique, distinguishable, irreplaceable entities is 'the elementary ideological effect' (161).

The obviousness of subjectivity as the origin of meaning and choice has been challenged by the linguistic theory which has developed on the basis of Saussure's. As Emile Benveniste argues, it is language which provides the possibility of subjectivity, because it is language which enables the speaker to posit himself or herself as 'I', as the subject of a sentence. It is in language, in other words, that people constitute themselves as subjects. Consciousness of self is possible only on the basis of differentiation: 'I' cannot be signified or conceived without the concep-

tion 'non-I', 'you', and dialogue, the fundamental condition of language,[3] implies a reversible polarity between 'I' and 'you'. 'Language is
possible only because each speaker sets himself up as a *subject* by referring to himself as I' (Benveniste 1971: 225). But if in language there are
only differences with no positive terms, as Saussure insists, 'I' designates
only the subject of a specific utterance. 'And so', Benveniste goes on,

> it is literally true that the basis of subjectivity is in the exercise of
> language. If one really thinks about it, one will see that there is no
> other testimony to the identity of the subject except that which he
> himself thus gives about himself.

> (226)

Within ideology, of course, it seems 'obvious' that the individual
speaker is the origin of the meaning of his or her utterance. Post-
Saussurean linguistics, however, implies a more complex relationship
between the individual and language, since it is language itself which,
by differentiating between concepts, offers the possibility of meaning.
In practice, it is only by taking up the position of the subject in language that the individual is able to produce meaning. Jacques Derrida
summarizes the issues:

> what was it that Saussure in particular reminded us of? That 'language
> [which consists only of differences] is not a function of the speaking
> subject'. This implies that the subject (self-identical or even conscious
> of self-identity, self-conscious) is inscribed in the language, that he is a
> 'function' of the language. He becomes a *speaking* subject only by
> conforming his speech . . . to the system of linguistic prescriptions
> taken as the system of differences. . . .

> (1973: 145–6)

Derrida goes on to raise the question whether, even if we accept that it
is only signifying practice that makes possible the speaking subject, we
can nevertheless conceive of a non-speaking, non-signifying subject,
present to itself as 'a silent and intuitive consciousness' (146). The
problem here, he concludes, is to define consciousness-in-itself, as
distinct from consciousness of something, and ultimately as distinct

from consciousness of self. If consciousness is in the end consciousness of self, this in turn implies that consciousness depends on differentiation, and specifically on Benveniste's differentiation between 'I' and 'you', a process made possible by language.

PSYCHOANALYSIS

The implications of this concept of the primacy of language over subjectivity have been developed in the course of Jacques Lacan's reading (rereading) of Freud. Subjectivity, in Lacanian theory, is not given, but acquired, and is sustained thereafter only with a degree of difficulty. Lacan's account of the subject as constructed in language confirms the *decentring* of consciousness so that it can no longer be seen as the origin of meaning, knowledge and action.

Instead, Lacan proposes that the infant is initially an 'hommelette' – 'a little man and also like a broken egg spreading without hindrance in all directions' (Coward and Ellis 1977: 101). The child has in the first instance no sense of identity, no way of conceiving of itself as a unit, distinct from what is 'other', exterior to it. During the 'mirror stage' of its development, however, it 'recognizes' itself in the mirror as a unity, and distinguishable from the outside world. The 'recognition' is an identification with an 'imaginary' self that is unitary and autonomous (Lacan 1977a: 1–7). This self is imaginary because imaged, and also because it is visible as a unit only in the mirror world, over there. The recognition is also a misrecognition.

But it is only with its entry into language that the child becomes a subject, capable of speech. If it is to participate in the society into which it is born, to be able to act deliberately within the social formation, the child must enter what Lacan calls the symbolic order, must submit, in other words, to the discipline of the signifying systems of culture, among which the supreme example is language. The child who refuses to learn its mother tongue is 'sick', unable to become a full member of the family and of society.

In order to speak, the child is compelled to differentiate; to speak of itself, it has to distinguish 'I' from 'you'. In order to define what it wants, the child learns to identify with the first person singular pronoun, and this identification constitutes the basis of subjectivity.

Subsequently, the child learns to recognize itself in a series of subject-positions ('he' or 'she', 'boy' or 'girl', and so on), which are the positions from which speech is intelligible to itself and others. Like the first, this recognition is also to a degree a misrecognition, a classification imposed not by nature, but by the Other (capital O), from outside.

Subjects are subjects of particular forms of knowledge, which may construct mutually incompatible subject-positions. 'Identity', subjectivity, is thus a matrix of subject-positions, which may be inconsistent, or even in contradiction with one another. The subject, then, is linguistically and discursively constructed and displaced across the range of knowledges in which the concrete individual participates. It follows from Saussure's theory of language as composed of differences that the world is intelligible only discursively: there is no unmediated experience, no direct access to the raw reality of self and others. Thus,

> As well as being a system of signs related among themselves, language incarnates meaning in the form of the series of positions it offers for the subject from which to grasp itself and its relations with the real.

> (Nowell-Smith 1976: 26)

The subject is constructed in language and, since the symbolic order constitutes the inscription of ideology, in ideology itself. It is in this sense that ideology has the effect, as Althusser argues, of constituting individuals as subjects, and it is also in this sense that their subjectivity appears 'obvious'. Ideology effaces the role of language in the constitution of the subject. As a result, people 'recognize' (misrecognize) themselves in the ways in which ideology 'interpellates' them or, in other words, addresses them as subjects, calls them by their names, and 'acknowledges' their autonomy. As a result, they 'work by themselves' (Althusser 1971: 169); they willingly adopt the subject-positions necessary to their participation in the social formation.

In capitalist societies subjects 'freely' exchange their labour-power for wages, and they 'choose' from the commodities produced. And it is here that we see the full force of Althusser's term 'subject', originally borrowed, as he says, from law. The subject is not only a grammatical subject, a centre of initiatives, author of and responsible for its actions, but also a *subjected being*, who submits to the authority of the social formation, represented in ideology as the Absolute Subject (God, the monarch, the boss, Man, consumerism, good taste, or conscience itself):

> the individual *is interpellated as a (free) subject in order that he shall submit freely to the commandments of the Subject, i.e. in order that he shall (freely) accept his subjection.*

> (Althusser 1971: 169)

RESISTANCE

So far the circle appears complete and closed, and it is difficult to account in theoretical terms for Althusser's belief in the possibility of class struggle, and the option of deliberate action to challenge the existing social formation. Ideology, after all, because it is more than a simple fiction, because it is inscribed in the language we learn from our earliest years, is not something we can simply dispense with in the same way as children discard Father Christmas when they no longer need him. Because ideology has the role of constituting individuals as subjects, because it is produced in the identification with the 'I' of language, and is thus the condition of deliberate action, we cannot simply step outside it. To do so would be to refuse to act or speak, and even to make such a refusal, to say 'I refuse', is to accept the condition of subjectivity.

How, then, can we resist the form of our own ideological interpellation? Ideology addresses concrete individuals as subjects, calls us into being, and at the same time calls us to account. Bourgeois ideology, in particular, stresses the fixed identity of the individual. 'I'm just like that', we explain; 'that's who I am' – indecisive, perhaps, or aggressive, generous or impulsive. Astrology is only an extreme form of the determinism which attributes to us given essences that cannot change and that account for our choices. Popular psychology and popular fiction make individual behaviour a product of these essences, the character-types of the nineteenth-century novel. And underlying them all, ultimately unalterable, is 'human nature'. In these circumstances, how is it possible to suppose that, even if we could break in theoretical terms with the concepts of the ruling ideology, we are ourselves capable of change, and capable in consequence of acting to change the social formation, and of transforming ourselves to form a new kind of society?

It is important to note that what is at stake here is the ruling ideology. For any Marxist, there is necessarily an alternative possibility, the revolutionary ideology of a class for itself, a class that refuses its own subjection and subscribes to another analysis of the options. But neither Marx nor Althusser supposed that the necessity of selling their labour-power would by itself make people revolutionary. If the ISAs are so pervasive, if they reach so deeply into everyday life, how is resistance thinkable?

A possible answer can be sought in psychoanalysis. Althusser's use of the term 'imaginary' owes something to Lacan's account of the mirror stage and the decentring of the subject. In Lacanian theory the individual is by no means the harmonious and coherent totality of ideological misrecognition. The mirror stage, in which the infant perceives itself as other, an image, exterior to its own perceiving self, produces a split between the I which is perceived in the mirror and the perceiving I that identifies with it. The entry into language necessitates a secondary division which reinforces the first, a split between the I that speaks and the I we speak of, between the subject of the enunciation, the speaker, on the one hand, and, on the other, the subject of the *énoncé*, the utterance (see p. 29 above). There is thus a distinction between the conscious subject represented in its own speech, and the subject which is only partly identifiable there, the subject that speaks.

In the gap formed by this division we may locate the unconscious. According to Lacan, the unconscious is constituted in the moment of entry into the symbolic order, at the same time as the construction of the subject. As the repository of the drives that impel the little human organism, repressed in obedience to the discipline imposed by language and culture, the unconscious is a constant source of potential disruption of that obedience.

DESIRE

Submission to the symbolic order releases the child into the possibility of social relationship; it reduces infantile helplessness to the extent that the child can now specify its needs and anxieties in the form of demands. But at the same time, while offering the possibility of formulating the child's wishes, the symbolic order also betrays them. In so far as our wants are subjected to the language which always precedes us, exists outside us, and is always, as Lacan puts it, Other (capital O), these wants return to us alienated, other than they are, and what is lost in the process survives as unconscious desire (Lacan 1977a: 286). What we ask for is not (exactly) what we want. Demand is never more than a metonymy of desire (Lemaire 1977: 64), its substitute, an adjunct that attempts and fails to take its place.

It follows that the Lacanian subject is a precarious creature, its identity borrowed from elsewhere, from the Other. The subject is perpetually in the process of construction and reconstruction, thrown into crisis by changes in language and the social formation; it is also able to learn new vocabularies, new analyses of the way things are. Driven by unconscious desire, moreover, the subject is restless, dissatisfied, and eager, if only in unrecognized ways, for change. And in that precariousness, that dissatisfaction, lies the possibility of transformation.

In addition, the displacement of subjectivity across a range of knowledges implies a range of positions from which the subject grasps itself and its relations with the real, and these positions, as I have suggested, may be incompatible or contradictory. The incompatibilities and contradictions within what is taken for granted also exert a pressure on concrete individuals to seek new, non-contradictory subject-positions, even if, in the event, no wholly non-contradictory place is available.

To take a familiar instance, women in our society are at once produced and inhibited by contradictory imperatives. Very broadly, women have access both to the liberal-humanist promise of freedom, self-determination and rationality, and at the same time to a specifically feminine ideal of submission, relative inadequacy and irrational intuition. The attempt to locate a single and coherent subject-position within these conflicting models, and in consequence to find a non-contradictory pattern of behaviour, can create intolerable pressures. One way of responding to this situation is to retreat from the contradictions, and from the language that defines the conflicting ideals, to become 'sick'. More women than men are treated for mental illness. Another way out is to seek a resolution of the contradictions in the politics of feminism. That the position of women in society has changed so slowly, in spite of such a radical instability in it, may be partly explained by the relative exclusion, at least until recently, of the feminine from the vocabulary and the corresponding practices of liberal humanism. This relative exclusion, evident in the predominance of men in powerful positions in our social institutions, was inscribed, for example, in the use of masculine terms as generic ('rational man', etc.).

Women are not an isolated case. The survival of racism in a multi-cultural society also produces contradictory subject-positions, which precipitate changes in social relations not only between whole ethnic and cultural groups, but between concrete individuals within those groups. Even at the conscious level, although this fact may itself be unconscious, the individual subject is not a unity, and in this lies the possibility of deliberate change.

This does not imply the reinstatement of individual subjects as the origin of change and changing knowledges. On the contrary, it insists on the concept of a dialectical relationship between concrete individuals and the language in which their subjectivity is constructed. In consequence, it also supports the concept of subjectivity as always in process.

LITERATURE

It is because subjectivity is not fixed that literary texts can have an important function. No one, I think, would suggest that literature alone could precipitate a crisis in the social formation. None the less, if we accept Lacan's analysis of the importance of language in the constitution of the subject, it becomes apparent that literature, as one of the most persuasive uses of language, may have an important influence on the ways people understand themselves and their relation to the real relations in which they live. The interpellation of the reader in the literary text could be argued to have a role in reinforcing the concepts of the world and of subjectivity which ensure that people 'work by themselves' in the social formation. On the other hand, certain literary modes could be seen to challenge these concepts, and to call into question the particular complex of imaginary relations between individuals and the real conditions of their existence which helps to reproduce the present relations of production.

THE SUBJECT AND THE TEXT

Althusser analyses the interpellation of the subject in the context of ideology in general; Benveniste, in discussing the relationship between language and subjectivity, is concerned with language in general. None the less, it readily becomes apparent that capitalism in particular needs subjects who work by themselves, who freely exchange their labour-power for wages. It is in the epoch of capitalism that ideology emphasizes the value of individual freedom, freedom of conscience and, of course, consumer choice in all the multiplicity of its forms. The ideology of liberal humanism assumes a world of non-contradictory (and therefore fundamentally unalterable) individuals whose unfettered consciousness is the origin of meaning, knowledge and action. It is in the interest of this ideology above all to suppress the role of language in the construction of the subject, and its own role in the interpellation of the subject, and to present the individual as a free, unified, autonomous subjectivity. Classic realism, still the dominant popular mode in literature, film and television drama, roughly coincides chronologically with the epoch of industrial capitalism. It performs, I wish to suggest, the work of ideology, not only in its representation of a world of consistent subjects who are the origin of meaning, knowledge and action, but also in offering the reader, as the position from which the text is most readily intelligible, the position of subject as the origin both of understanding and of action in accordance with that understanding.

It is readily apparent that Romantic and post-Romantic poetry, from Wordsworth through the Victorian period at least to Eliot and Yeats, takes subjectivity as its central theme. The developing self of the poet, his consciousness of himself as poet, his struggle against the constraints of an outer reality, constitute the preoccupations of *The Prelude, In Memoriam* or *Meditations in Time of Civil War*. The 'I' of these poems is a kind of super-subject, experiencing life at a higher level of intensity than ordinary people and absorbed in a world of selfhood which the phenomenal world, perceived as external and antithetical, either nourishes or constrains. This transcendence of the subject in poetry is not presented as unproblematic, as I shall suggest in Chapter 6, but it is entirely overt in the poetry of this period. The 'I' of the poem directly addresses an individual reader who is invited to respond equally directly to this interpellation.

Fiction, however, in this same period, frequently appears to deal rather in social relationships, the interaction between the individual and society, to the increasing exclusion of the subjectivity of the author. Direct intrusion by the author comes to seem an impropriety; impersonal narration, 'showing' (the truth) rather than 'telling' it, is a requirement of prose fiction by the end of the nineteenth century. In drama too the author is apparently absent from the self-contained fictional world on the stage. Even the text effaces its own existence as text: unlike poetry, which clearly announces itself as formal, if only in terms of the shape of the text on the page, the novel seems merely to transcribe a series of events, to report on a palpable world, however fictional. Classic realist drama displays transparently and from the outside how people speak and behave.

Nevertheless, as we know while we read or watch, the author is present as a shadowy authority and as source of the fiction, and the author's presence is substantiated by the name on the cover or the programme: 'a novel by Thomas Hardy', 'a new play by Ibsen'. And at the same time, as I shall suggest in this section, the form of the classic realist text acts in conjunction with the expressive theory and with ideology by interpellating the reader as subject. The reader is invited to perceive and judge the 'truth' of the text, the coherent, non-contradictory interpretation of the world as it is perceived by an author whose autonomy is the source and evidence of the truth of the interpretation. This model of intersubjective communication, of shared understanding of a text which re-presents the world, is the guarantee not only of the truth of the text but of the reader's existence as an autonomous and knowing subject in a world of knowing subjects. In this way classic realism constitutes an ideological practice in addressing itself to readers as subjects, interpellating them in order that they freely accept their subjectivity and their subjection.

It is important to reiterate, of course, that this process is not inevitable, in the sense that texts do not determine, like fate, the ways in which they *must* be read. I am concerned at this stage primarily with ways in which they are conventionally read: conventionally, since language is conventional, and since modes of writing as well as ways of reading are conventional, but conventionally also in that new conventions of reading are available, as I shall suggest in Chapter 6. In this sense meaning is never a fixed essence inherent in the text but is always constructed by the reader, the result of a 'circulation' between social formation, reader and text (Heath 1977–8: 74). In the same way, 'inscribed subject positions are never hermetically sealed into a text, but are always positions in ideologies' (Willemen 1978: 63). To argue that classic realism interpellates subjects in certain ways is not to propose that this process is ineluctable: on the contrary it is a matter of choice. But the choice is ideological: certain ranges of meaning (there is always room for debate) are 'obvious' within the currently dominant ideology, and certain subject-positions are equally 'obviously' the positions from which these meanings are apparent.

In what follows I have drawn very freely on work on film in *Screen* magazine, probably one of the most important sources for the development of critical theory in Britain. I have not always attributed specific insights and I have not hesitated to adapt others. The debate in *Screen* was more complex and subtle than it is possible to indicate in an argument which inevitably modifies and abridges much of what it borrows.

Classic realism is characterized by *illusionism*, narrative which leads to *closure*, and a *hierarchy of voices* which establishes the 'truth' of the story. Illusionism is by now, I hope, self-explanatory. The other two defining characteristics of classic realism need some discussion. Narrative tends to follow certain recurrent patterns. Classic realist narrative, as Barthes demonstrates in S/Z, turns on the creation of enigma through the precipitation of disorder, which throws into disarray the conventional cultural and signifying systems. Among the commonest sources of disorder at the level of plot in classic realism are murder, war, a journey or love. But the story moves inevitably towards *closure* which is also disclosure, the dissolution of enigma through the re-establishment of order, recognizable as a reinstatement or a development of the order which is understood to have preceded the events of the story itself.

The moment of closure is the point at which the events of the story become fully intelligible to the reader. The most obvious instance is the detective story where, in the final pages, the murderer is revealed and the motive made plain. But a high degree of intelligibility is sustained throughout the narrative as a result of the *hierarchy of voices* in the text. The hierarchy works above all by means of a privileged voice which places as subordinate all the utterances that are literally or figuratively between inverted commas. Colin MacCabe illustrates this point by quoting a passage from George Eliot (MacCabe 1974: 9–10). Here is another. It concerns Mr Tulliver, who has determined to call in the money he has lent his sister, Mrs Moss. They are discussing Mrs Moss's four daughters who have, as she puts it, 'a brother a-piece':

> 'Ah, but they must turn out and fend for themselves,' said Mr Tulliver, feeling that his severity was relaxing, and trying to brace it by throwing out a wholesome hint. 'They mustn't look to hanging on their brothers.'
>
> 'No; but I hope their brothers 'ull love the poor things, and remember they came o' one father and mother: the lads 'ull never be the poorer for that,' said Mrs Moss, flashing out with hurried timidity, like a half-smothered fire.
>
> Mr Tulliver gave his horse a little stroke on the flank, then checked it, and said angrily, 'Stand still with you!' much to the astonishment of that innocent animal.
>
> 'And the more there is of 'em, the more they must love one another,' Mrs Moss went on, looking at her children with a didactic purpose. But she turned towards her brother again to say, 'Not but what I hope your boy 'ull allays be good to his sister, though there's but two of 'em, like you and me, brother.'
>
> That arrow went straight to Mr Tulliver's heart. He had not a rapid imagination, but the thought of Maggie was very near to him, and he was not long in seeing his relation to his own sister side by side with

> Tom's relation to Maggie. Would the little wench ever be poorly off, and Tom rather hard upon her?
>
> 'Ay, ay, Gritty,' said the miller, with a new softness in his tone; 'but I've allays done what I could for you,' he added, as if vindicating himself from a reproach.
>
> *(The Mill on the Floss*, Chapter 8)

The distinction here between the dialogue and the authorial and therefore authoritative exposition of its psychological import illustrates the distinction made by Benveniste between 'discourse' and 'history' (*histoire*) (Benveniste 1971: 205–15). History narrates events apparently without the intervention of a speaker. In history there is no mention of 'you' and 'I'; 'the events seem to narrate themselves' (p. 208). Discourse, on the other hand, acknowledges a voice; it assumes a speaker and a hearer, the 'you' and 'I' of dialogue. In third-person narrative fiction like *The Mill on the Floss* the voices are placed for the reader by a privileged, historic narration which is the source of coherence of the story as a whole. Here Mr Tulliver is more aware of the 'truth' of the situation than Mrs Moss – we know this because the fact has previously been related as history: 'If Mrs Moss had been one of the most astute women in the world, instead of being one of the simplest, she could have thought of nothing more likely to propitiate her brother. . .'. But he has less access to the 'truth' than the reader, whose comprehensive understanding is guaranteed by the historic narration: '. . . he was not long in seeing his relation to his own sister side by side with Tom's relation to Maggie. . . .' The authority of this impersonal narration springs from its effacement of its own status as discourse.

At the same time the passage is interesting as an example of the way in which the reader is invited to *construct* a 'history' which is more comprehensive still. The gently ironic account of Mr Tulliver's treatment of his horse is presented without overt authorial comment. The context, however, points more or less irresistibly to a single interpretation which appears as the product of an intersubjective communication between the author and the reader in which the role of language has become invisible. Irony is no less authoritative because its meanings are implicit rather than explicit. Indeed, the frequent overt authorial intrusions and generalizations of George Eliot are much easier to resist, since they draw attention to themselves as propositions. First-person narration, therefore, or the presentation of events through the perceptions of centres of consciousness within the fiction, however 'unreliable', are not necessarily ways of evading authorial authority. But they seem to offer the reader a meaning which is apparently not in the words on the page. Through the presentation of an intelligible history which effaces its own status as discourse, classic realism proposes a model in which author and reader are subjects who are the source of shared meanings, the origin of which is mysteriously extra-discursive. It thus does the work of ideology in suppressing the relationship between language and subjectivity.

Classic realism, then, is what Barthes in S/Z defines as the readable (*lisible*), the dominant literary form of the nineteenth century, no longer 'pertinent' since then and yet still the prevailing form of popular fiction today, the accomplice of ideology in its attempt to arrest the productivity of literary practice. Classic realism tends to offer as the 'obvious' basis of its intelligibility the assumption that character, unified and coherent, is the source of action. Subjectivity is a major – perhaps the major – theme of classic realism. Insight into character and psychological processes is declared to be one of the marks of serious literature: 'it is largely the victory of character over action that distinguishes the high literature of modern times' (Langbaum 1963: 210).

Conversely, inconsistency of character or the inappropriateness of particular actions to particular characters is seen as a weakness. It is because Emma is the kind of person she is that she behaves as she does; Sir Willoughby Patterne acts as he does because he is an egoist. Whether influenced by family relationships and upbringing, or simply mysteriously given, character begins to manifest itself in the earliest years of Maggie Tulliver, Jane Eyre and Paul Morel, for instance, and it proves a major constraint on their future development, on the choices they make and the courses they pursue.

In the more arbitrary world portrayed in earlier literary forms, pairs of characters, barely distinguishable from each other except by name, demonstrate the differences that result from circumstances and accidents of choice. Palamon and Arcite, Helena and Hermia, Rosalind and Celia seem to have everything in common except their destinies (and in the last two cases their physical heights). If pairs of characters appear in classic realist texts, however, it is more often with the effect of showing how the differences of character between them are the source of their differing destinies. When Dorothea rejects Sir James Chettam and Celia marries him, their respective actions are seen as consistent with the character-patterns established for them at length in the opening pages of Middlemarch. Elinor and Marianne Dashwood are naturally different, and if Marianne acquires at nineteen the sense that she lacked at seventeen, it is at the price of a considerable period of illness and convalescence.

The illness marking such adjustments of character was to become a convention of nineteenth-century fiction and the problem of change it symbolizes forms a striking contrast to the rapid transformations of, for instance, Shakespeare's erring prodigals, Prince Hal, Angelo and Bertram, who are able to enter so promptly into the possession of virtue, a quantity equally and readily available to all repentant sinners. Their tragic counterparts in Renaissance drama fall equally readily into vice: Faustus, Beatrice-Joanna and Macbeth need not be understood as *characteristically* depraved, though a mode of criticism based on the dominance of classic realist literature has until recently been inclined to analyse them in terms appropriate to the novel. If Lawrence did indeed do away with 'the old stable ego of the character', it was in search of a deeper form of subjectivity that he did so. It is difficult to imagine Miriam becoming like Clara, Gudrun like Ursula or Gerald like Birkin. Equally, the overt project of The Mill on the Floss is most 'obviously' intelligible in terms of a difference of character between Tom and Maggie.

Classic realism presents individuals whose traits of character, understood as essential, constrain the choices they make, and whose potential for development depends on what is given. Human nature is thus seen as a system of character-differences existing in the world, but one which none the less permits the reader to share the hopes and fears of a wide range of kinds of characters. This contradiction – that readers, like the central figures of fiction, are unique, and that so many readers can identify with so many protagonists – is accommodated in ideology as a paradox. There is no character in Middlemarch with whom we cannot have some sense of shared humanity. In Heart of Darkness, Marlow is

Catherine Belsey, *Critical Practice*, second edition (London: Routledge, 2002).

appalled to find in the jungles of the Congo a recognition of his own remote kinship with primeval savagery: 'And why not? The mind of man is capable of anything – because everything is in it, all the past as well as all the future' (Section 2). 'The mind of man', infinite and infinitely mysterious, homogeneous system of differences, unchangeable in its essence however manifold its forms, is shown in classic realism to be the source of understanding, of action and of history.

The consistency and continuity of the subject provides the conceptual framework of classic realism, but it is characteristic of the action of the story, the narrative process itself, to disrupt subjectivity, to disturb the pattern of relationships between subject-positions which is presented as normal in the text. In many cases the action itself represents a test of identity, putting identity in question by confronting the protagonist with alternative possible actions. In others a murder, marital infidelity, a journey, or the arrival of a stranger commonly disrupts the existing system of differences which constitutes human nature as represented in the microcosm of the text. To this extent classic realism recognizes the precariousness of the ego and offers the reader the sense of danger and excitement which results from that recognition.

But the movement of classic realist narrative towards closure ensures the reinstatement of order, sometimes a new order, sometimes the old restored, but always intelligible because familiar. Decisive choices are made, identity is established, the murderer is exposed, or marriage generates a new set of subject-positions. The epilogue common in nineteenth-century novels describes the new order, now understood to be static, and thus isolates and emphasizes a structural feature which is left implicit in other classic realist texts. Jane Eyre tells her readers, 'My tale draws to its close: one word respecting my experience of married life, and one brief glance at the fortunes of those whose names have most frequently recurred in this narrative, and I have done' (Chapter 38). Harmony has been re-established through the redistribution of the signifiers into a new system of differences which closes off the threat to subjectivity, and it remains only to make this harmonious and coherent world intelligible to the reader, closing off in the process the sense of danger to the reader's subjectivity. This characteristic narrative structure, which deserves more detailed exposition, is discussed in the context of a full analysis of the film, *Touch of Evil*, in Stephen Heath's 'Film and System: Terms of Analysis' (1975).

Jane Eyre addresses itself to the reader, directly interpellates the reader as subject, as the 'you' who is addressed by the 'I' of discourse. This interpellation (address) in turn facilitates the interpolation (inclusion) of the reader in the narrative by the presentation of events from a specific and unified point of view. The meeting between Odysseus and Nausicaa in *The Odyssey*, or the death of Priam in *The Aeneid*, provide no specific position in the scene for the reader. But classic realism locates the reader in the events: we seem to 'see' Mr Brocklehurst through the eyes of Jane as a child:

> I looked up at – a black pillar! – such, at least, appeared to me, at first sight, the straight, narrow, sable-clad shape standing erect on the rug: the grim face at the top was like a carved mask, placed above the shaft by way of capital.
>
> (Chapter 4)

Besides emphasizing the concern of the text with subjectivity, this technique also limits the play of meaning for the reader by installing him or her in a single position from which the scene is intelligible. This is not an inevitable consequence of first person narrative – Aeneas recounts the death of Priam – nor is it confined to that particular form. Here is an episode from *Oliver Twist*:

> The undertaker, who had just put up the shutters of his shop, was making some entries in his day-book by the light of a most dismal candle, when Mr Bumble entered.
>
> 'Aha!' said the undertaker, looking up from the book, and pausing in the middle of a word; 'is that you, Bumble?'
>
> 'No one else, Mr Sowerberry,' replied the beadle. 'Here. I've brought the boy.' Oliver made a bow.
>
> 'Oh! that's the boy, is it?' said the undertaker, raising the candle above his head, to get a better view of Oliver. 'Mrs Sowerberry, will you have the goodness to come here a moment, my dear?'
>
> Mrs Sowerberry emerged from a little room behind the shop, and

presented the form of a short, thin, squeezed-up woman with a vixen-
ish countenance.

'My dear,' said Mr Sowerberry deferentially, 'this is the boy from the
workhouse that I told you of.' Oliver bowed again.

'Dear me!' said the undertaker's wife, 'he's very small.'

(Chapter 4)

The scene (since again the narrative is full of visual detail) is viewed
from a quite specific point of view, just inside the door of the shop. The
raising of the candle, the emergence of Mrs Sowerberry and her
appearance are all 'presented' to this single place, the place of Oliver,
who is the centre of consciousness of the episode. We 'see' what Oliver
sees, and to this extent we identify with him. But we also see more than
Oliver sees: we are aware of his bow, narrated in the third person; we
know that the undertaker has just put up the shutters, and that he
pauses in the middle of a word.

This information has no obvious place in Oliver's consciousness,
and the more comprehensive point of view that it permits the reader
sets up a tripartite relationship between the reader, the fictional
character and the implied author. The reader participates not only in
the point of view of the subject of the énoncé, the subject inscribed in the
utterance, Oliver, but also in the point of view of the subject of the
enunciation, the subject who narrates, who 'shows' Oliver's experience to the reader, the implied author. In a similar way the conventional
tenses of classic realism tend to align the position of the reader with
that of the omniscient narrator who is looking back on a series of past
events. Thus, while each episode seems to be happening 'now' as we
read, and the reader is given clear indications of what is already past in
relation to this 'now', nonetheless each apparently present episode is
contained in a single, intelligible and all-embracing vision of what,
from the point of view of the subject of the enunciation, is past and
completed.

In this way heterogeneity – variety of points of view and temporal
locations – is contained in homogeneity. The text interpellates the
reader as a transcendent and noncontradictory subject by positioning
him or her as 'the unified and unifying subject of its vision' (Heath
1976: 85).

This construction of a position for the reader, which is a position of identification with the subject of the enunciation, is by no means confined to third-person narrative, where authorial omniscience is so readily apparent. In distinguishing between 'reliable' and 'unreliable' first person narrators, the reader assumes a position of knowledge – of a history, a 'truth' of the story which may not be accessible to a dramatized narrator who, as a character in the text, is a subject of the *énoncé*. Jane Eyre as a child often has less understanding of the implications of her experience than the reader does. In *Wuthering Heights* the inadequacies of the perceptions of Lockwood or Nellie Dean do not prevent the reader from seeming to apprehend the real nature of the relationship between Catherine and Heathcliff.

Browning's dramatic monologues, to cite an extreme example, invite the reader to make judgements and draw conclusions not available to the speaker. Robert Langbaum perfectly describes the common reading experience in which the knowledge of the reader seems to surpass the knowledge of the speaker, but to be a knowledge shared with the author, so that author and reader independently produce a shared meaning which confirms the transcendence of each:

> It can be said of the dramatic monologue generally that there is at work in it a consciousness, whether intellectual or historical, beyond what the speaker can lay claim to. This consciousness is the mark of the poet's projection into the poem; and it is also the pole which attracts our projection, since we find in it the counterpart of our own consciousness.
>
> (Langbaum 1963: 94)

Irony thus guarantees still more effectively than overt authorial omniscience the subjectivity of the reader as a source of meaning.

The dramatic monologue is compelled by the logic of its form to leave the recognition of irony to the reader. The classic realist novel, however, has a surer way of establishing its harmonious 'truth'.[4] Perhaps the commonest pattern in the novel is the gradual convergence of the voices of the subject of the *énoncé* and the subject of the enunciation until they merge triumphantly at the point of closure. At the end of the detective story, reader, author and detective all 'know' everything

necessary to the intelligibility of the story. Nineteenth-century protagonists learn by experience until they achieve the wisdom author and
reader now seem to have possessed all along. (Paradoxically the protagonist's discovery also has the effect of confirming the wisdom of the
reader.) Wayne Booth describes the position of the reader who has
completed *Emma*:

> 'Jane Austen' has learned nothing at the end of the novel that she did
> not know at the beginning. She needed to learn nothing. She knew
> everything of importance already. We have been privileged to watch
> with her as she observes her favorite character climb from a consider-
> ably lower platform to join the exalted company of Knightley, 'Jane
> Austen', and those of us readers who are wise enough, good enough,
> and perceptive enough to belong up there too.
>
> (Booth 1961: 265).

Bleak House must be one of the most interesting instances of
converging voices. The story itself concerns social and ideological contradictions – that the law of property set up in the interests of society
benefits only lawyers and destroys the members of society who invoke
it in their defence; that the social conception of virtue promotes hypo-
crisy or distress. The narrative mode of *Bleak House* also functions contradictorily, initially liberating the reader to produce meaning but
finally proving to be a constraint on the process of production. The
novel has two narrators, Esther Summerson, innocent, generous,
unassuming and sentimental, and an anonymous third-person narrator,
detached, ironic, rendered cynical by what he knows about the Court
of Chancery. Neither is omniscient. The anonymous narration is in the
present tense, and claims little knowledge of feeling. At the beginning
of *Bleak House* the two narratives form a striking contrast. The first section is by the worldly, knowing narrator, and is succeeded by Esther's
immediate insistence on her own lack of cleverness but strength of
feeling: 'I have not by any means a quick understanding. When I love a
person very tenderly indeed, it seems to brighten . . .' (Chapter 3).

The reader is constantly prompted to supply the deficiencies of each
narrative. The third person narration, confining itself largely to
behaviour, is strongly enigmatic, but provides enough clues for the

reader to make guesses at the 'truth' before the story reveals it; Esther's narrative frequently invites an ironic reading: we are encouraged to trust her account of the 'facts' but not necessarily her judgement:

> She was a good, good woman. She went to church three times every Sunday, and to morning prayers on Wednesdays and Fridays, and to lectures whenever there were lectures; and never missed. She was handsome; and if she had ever smiled, would have been (I used to think) like an angel – but she never smiled. She was always grave, and strict. She was so very good herself, I thought, that the badness of other people made her frown all her life. . . . It made me very sorry to consider how good she was, and how unworthy of her I was.
>
> (Chapter 3)

Thus, a third and privileged but literally unwritten story begins to emerge, recounted by the reader, who grasps a history and judges soundly.

Gradually, however, the three narratives converge. The childlike spontaneity of Mr Skimpole, which enchanted Esther in Chapter 6, and which rapidly emerges as irresponsibility in the narrative of the reader, is dismissed by Esther in Chapter 61 with a briskness worthy of the ironic narrator:

> He died some five years afterwards, and left a diary behind him, with letters and other material towards his Life; which was published, and which showed him to have been the victim of a combination on the part of mankind against an amiable child. It was considered very pleasant reading, but I never read more of it myself than the sentence on which I chanced to light on opening the book. It was this. 'Jarndyce, in common with most other men I have known, is the Incarnation of Selfishness.'

It is Esther, and not the ironic narrator, who recounts the black comedy of the completion of the case of Jarndyce and Jarndyce, while the anonymous narrative softens, as if as a result of its encounters with the innocence of Jo, the crossing-sweeper, the Bagnet family and Mr George:

> A goodly sight it is to see the grand old housekeeper (harder of hear-
> ing now) going to church on the arm of her son, and to observe –
> which few do, for the house is scant of company in these times – the
> relations of both towards Sir Leicester, and his towards them.
>
> (Chapter 66)

The three narratives thus converge to confirm the reader's apparently extra-discursive interpretation and judgement.

By this means, Bleak House constructs a reality which appears to be many-sided, too complex to be contained within a single point of view, but which is in fact so contained within the single and non-contradictory invisible narrative of the reader, which is confirmed and ratified as Esther and the ironic narrator come to share with the reader a 'recognition' of the true complexity of things. By thus smoothing over the contradictions it has so powerfully dramatized in the interests of a single, unified, coherent 'truth', – Bleak House, however critical of the world it describes, offers the reader a position, an attitude which is given as non-contradictory, fixed in 'knowing' subjectivity.

Classic realism cannot foreground contradiction. The logic of its structure – the movement towards closure – precludes the possibility of leaving the reader simply to confront the contradictions which the text may have defined. The hierarchy of voices ensures that a transcendent level of knowledge 'recognizes' the contradictions in the world as tragic (inevitable), as is predominantly the case in Hardy, or ironic, as in Bleak House, or resolved as in Sybil or Jane Eyre. When contradiction exists in classic realism it does so in the margins of a text which, as Pierre Macherey argues in A Theory of Literary Production (1978), is unable, in spite of itself, to achieve the coherence which is the project of classic realism.

It may prove persuasive to rehearse some of the preceding arguments very briefly in relation to a single text. Henry James's What Maisie Knew is a story about degrees of knowing: it is precisely an analysis of subjectivity. Maisie's subjectivity is given. She becomes sharper, more acute in the course of the novel, but her radical innocence, integrity and sensitivity are understood to be simply there and unalterable, just as the weakness of Sir Claude is there and cannot be changed, however hard anyone, including Sir Claude, tries to change it. The shallow, self-seeking natures of Ida, Beale and Mrs Beale are also given, and the novel is intelligible in terms of a concept of human nature as a system of differences existing in the world. Society can exert its influence only on what is understood to be natural and essential, and in the case of Maisie herself this influence is powerless to corrupt her.

The action of the novel constitutes above all a test of Maisie's identity. There are events, but the climax of the events is climactic as the test of Maisie's nature, her subjectivity. What is presented as supremely important is what Maisie *is*.

The hierarchy of voices is readily apparent. The narration is in the third person, presented largely but by no means entirely through Maisie as a centre of consciousness. The superficial voice of the fashionable world is patently shallow, over-emotional, inadequate; the imperative moral voice of Mrs Wix is in a kind of symmetry with the sensitive but ineffectual voice of Sir Claude. Maisie subsumes both, transcending the 'moral sense' of Mrs Wix and able to participate in the self-awareness of Sir Claude's 'fear of himself' without succumbing to it. Not 'knowing' in the worldly sense the clinical facts of sex, Maisie 'knows' at a level which is seen as more profound.

But beyond this hierarchy of knowledge within the *énoncé*, the irony constructs a knowing position for the reader, who suspects Mrs Beale of falsehood from the moment she is introduced into the text (as Miss Overmore):

> Miss Overmore never, like Moddle, had on an apron, and when she ate she held her fork with her little finger curled out. The child, who watched her at many moments, watched her particularly at that one. 'I think you're lovely,' she often said to her; even mamma, who was lovely too, had not such a pretty way with the fork.
>
> (Chapter 2)

The events which Maisie perceives but initially misinterprets or misjudges are intelligible to the reader, so that at the moment of closure, when Mrs Beale is unequivocally revealed by Maisie as predatory and destructive, *énoncé* and enunciation converge to produce an intersubjective consensus which confirms at once the autonomy of the reader, Maisie and Henry James as sources of recognition of the 'truth'.

The social comment which the text makes explicit is thus placed: the scandal of the child as an object of exchange is contained within the transcendent position of knowledge constructed for the reader, a position which is in itself non-contradictory and which is seen as the guarantee of moral autonomy, immunity from contamination by a corrupt society.

Initially (and continuously) constructed in language, the subject finds in the classic realist text a confirmation of the position of autonomous subjectivity represented in ideology as 'obvious'. It is possible to refuse that position, but to do so, at least at present, is to make a deliberate and ideological choice.

5

THE INTERROGATIVE TEXT

THE SPLIT SUBJECT

In Lacanian theory entry into language is necessary to the child unless he or she is to become 'sick'; at the same time entry into language inevitably creates a division between the subject of the enunciation and the subject of the *énoncé*, the 'I' who speaks and the 'I' who is represented in the utterance. The subject is held in place in the speech by the use of 'I', but this 'I' is always a 'stand-in' (Miller 1977–8: 25–6), a substitute for the 'I' who speaks. It is this contradiction in the subject – between the conscious self, which is conscious in so far as it is able to feature in language, and the self which is only partially represented there – which constitutes the source of possible change. The child's submission to the discursive practices of society is challenged by the existence of another self, which is not synonymous with the subject of its utterance.

For this reason it is in the interests of the stability of a class society, that is, it is in the interests of the reproduction of the existing relations of production, to suppress the contradiction in the subject, and it is this process of suppression which, I have argued, characterizes the classic realist text. The epoch of classic realism coincides roughly with the epoch of industrial capitalism. But at times of crisis in the social formation, when the mode of production is radically threatened, for instance, or in transition, confidence in the ideology of subjectivity is eroded. It is apparent in modern literature in some experimental forms and in certain films, but it can also be seen in some of the literature of the period of transition from feudalism to capitalism, where a major change in economic practice is accompanied by the equally major shift in ideological practice which we call the Renaissance.

Here, where nineteenth-century criticism so readily 'recognized' the rounded characters of classic realism, it is also possible, on the basis of a different critical approach, to find cases where the text permits the reader to glimpse a division within the subject. Jean-Marie Benoist finds an instance in Donne's 'Hymm to God my God, in my Sickness', which dramatizes in the text a distinction between the subject of the *énoncé* and the subject of the enunciation (Benoist 1971: 745–7):

> Since I am coming to that holy room,
>   Where, with thy choir of saints for evermore,
> I shall be made thy music; as I come
>   I tune the instrument here at the door,
>   And what I must do then, think here before.
>
> Whilst my physicians by their love are grown
>   Cosmographers, and I their map, who lie
> Flat on this bed, that by them may be shown
>   That this is my south-west discovery
>   *Per fretum febris*, by these straits to die,
>
> I joy, that in these straits, I see my west;
>   For, though their currents yield return to none,
> What shall my west hurt me? As west and east
>   In all flat maps (and I am one) are one,
>   So death doth touch the resurrection.

Here the speaker of the poem is both active and inert, instrument and tuner, dying and watching himself die. Though the recognition of this contradiction is facilitated by the Christian paradox of death as the passage to a higher form of life, and of human beings as participants in both this world ('map') and eternity, the division dramatized is not simply the dualist distinction between soul and body, or between a transitory and an immortal self. The subject who speaks actively watches himself *made* God's music in the future, by divine love, as he is now *made* a map through the care of the physicians. The subject of the poem is decentred, divided between the source of action (watching, tuning, joying) and the effect of action (music, map).

The contradiction is made apparent and startling by the use of the present tense. In narrative a distinction between a past 'I' and a present 'I' is common. Wordsworth's *Prelude* provides an instance of a direct contrast with Donne's poem. Here the project of the text is to ensure a convergence between the subject of the *énoncé* and the subject of the enunciation to create a unified identity which is intelligible as the product of past experience: what the poet *was*, we are to understand, is the source of what he *is*. Thus the narrative passages employ the past tense and there is a clear transition from narrative to meditation in the present tense:

> I would stand
> Beneath some rock, listening to sounds that are
> The ghostly language of the ancient earth,
> Or make their dim abode in distant winds.
> Thence did I drink the visionary power.
> I deem not profitless those fleeting moods
> Of shadowy exultation: not for this,
> That they are kindred to our purer mind
> And intellectual life; but that the soul,
> Remembering how she felt, but what she felt
> Remembering not, retains an obscure sense
> Of possible sublimity. . . .

(*The Prelude*, 1805, II, 326–37)

The split subject also appears in Renaissance drama, not merely in a state of inner conflict, which is common to Elizabethan tragedy and classic realism, but represented in a form which permits the audience to glimpse the concept of a division in subjectivity itself. Shakespeare's Richard III on the eve of the Battle of Bosworth wakes in fear from a dream which prophesies his death:

What do I fear? Myself? There's none else by.
Richard loves Richard; that is, I am I.
Is there a murderer here? No – yes; I am.
Then fly. What, from myself? Great reason why
Lest I revenge. What, myself upon myself!
Alack, I love myself. Wherefore? For any good
That I myself have done unto myself?
O, no. Alas, I rather hate myself
For hateful deeds committed by myself!
I am a villain; yet I lie, I am not.

(Richard III, V, iii, 182–91)

The syntax in which the self is seen as both subject and object, the assertions ('I am I') and the contradictions ('No – yes', 'I lie, I am not') all point to a disruption of the unified subject which is the source of meaning and action. Throughout the play Richard has been presented as identifying fully with the subject of his own utterance, 'I am determined to prove a villain' (I, i, 30). This identification with the subject of the *énoncé*, which in Lacan is the condition of deliberate action in the social formation, is the origin of Richard's behaviour in the play. But on the eve of Bosworth the subject of the utterance confronts the subject of the enunciation, which in a moment of crisis refuses to identify with Richard as agent of a series of murders: 'I am a villain; yet I lie, I am not.' It is a crisis of subjectivity which presents itself to the audience as a possible source of change – in Elizabethan terms a source of the repentance which is perpetually available to sinners, however hardened.

I emphasize these examples in order to urge that unity and consistency of character, the 'obvious' basis of intelligibility of classic realism, are not obvious to Renaissance readers and audiences. Brecht, who preserved an extremely ambivalent attitude to Renaissance drama, may have been drawn to it partly because of a common, or perhaps overlapping, concept of the subject as continuously in the process of construction. In Brecht's language,

> Even when a character behaves by contradictions that's only because nobody can be identically the same at two unidentical moments. . . .

> The continuity of the ego is a myth. A man is an atom that perpetually
> breaks up and forms anew.
>
> (Brecht 1964: 15)

In *Macbeth* the discontinuity of the ego and the explicit division of the
subject have become a structural principle of the play. Here the ethical
and ideological norms of loyalty, kinship and hospitality are set against
the 'black and deep desires' of the protagonist, which seem to come to
the surface at the beginning of the play and to escape rational control.
Macbeth, loyal and unified *subject* of a king who stands for these ideological (and discursive) norms, becomes a regicide in defiance of his
stated beliefs ('I have no spur. . . .' I, vii, 25) and in the process
destroys his own capacity to participate meaningfully in the symbolic
order of language and culture.

The imagery of the soliloquies externalizes the desires, which seem
to present themselves to consciousness as independent utterances invit-
ing consent: 'why do I yield to that suggestion/Whose horrid image
doth unfix my hair . . . ?' (I, iii, 134–5); and the process of temptation
explicitly destroys the unity of the self. 'My thought . . . shakes so my
single state of man . . .'(I, iii, 138–9). Macbeth consents to the sugges-
tion, identifies with the perpetrator of his actions and cements the
division of his own subjectivity: 'To know my deed, 'twere best not
know myself' (II, ii, 73). He becomes increasingly isolated from other
people, and his speech, confined to 'bloody instructions' is not able to
give meaning to the world, which comes to seem 'a tale/Told by an
idiot . . . signifying nothing' (V, v, 26–8). He has refused the subject-
positions offered him by the symbolic order and in consequence meaning eludes him; he has fallen into non-meaning (cf. Lacan 1977b:
211).

The metaphor of a shaken *state* (of man), of insurrection in the social
formation, is perhaps not wholly coincidental. *Macbeth* is a political play;
but more than that, the metaphor points outward to the parallel
between crisis in the social formation and the subject in crisis. The
transformation taking place in the Elizabethan economy is accompanied by glimpses in discursive practice of the subject as a process
rather than a fixity.

UNFIXING THE SUBJECT

The work of ideology is to present the position of the subject as fixed and unchangeable, an element in a given system of differences which is human nature and the world of human experience, and to show possible action as an endless repetition of 'normal', familiar action. To the extent that the classic realist text performs this work, classic realism is an ideological practice. But not all texts are classic realist texts, smoothing over contradiction in the construction of a position for the reader which is unified and knowing. Benveniste defines three kinds of utterance, synonymous with the three modalities of which the sentence is capable:

> it is everywhere recognized that there are declarative statements, interrogative statements, and imperative statements, which are distinguished by specific features of syntax and grammar although they are based in identical fashion upon predication. Now these three modalities do nothing but reflect the three fundamental behaviours of man speaking and acting through discourse upon his interlocutor: he wishes to impart a piece of knowledge to him or to obtain some information from him or to give an order to him. These are the three inter-human functions of discourse that are imprinted in the three modalities of the sentence-unit, each one corresponding to an attitude of the speaker.
>
> (Benveniste 1971: 110)

Benveniste's distinction between three fundamental functions of speech may be used, I want to suggest, to distinguish three kinds of texts, *declarative*, *imperative* and *interrogative*.

Classic realism clearly conforms to the modality Benveniste calls *declarative*, imparting 'knowledge' to a reader whose position is thereby stabilized, by a privileged narrative which is to varying degrees invisible. The *imperative* text, giving orders to its readers, is what is commonly thought of as 'propaganda'. Propaganda, it might be argued, is not obviously a distinct category, if it is accepted that classic realism is an ideological practice, but Steve Neale, in an excellent analysis of the possibility of isolating propagandist discourse, concludes that it is differentiated formally by a mode of address which invites the reader to adopt a position of struggle rather than stability, specifically struggle vis-à-vis something which is marked in the text as non-fictional, as existing outside discourse, in the world – sin, the Conservative Party, Russia. The imperative text – the sermon, party political broadcast or (in some cases) documentary film – aligns the reader 'as in identification with one set of discourses and practices and as in opposition to others . . . maintaining that identification and opposition, and . . . not resolving it but rather holding it as the position of closure' (Neale 1977: 31). Propaganda thus exhorts, instructs, orders the reader, constituting the reader as a unified subject in conflict with what exists outside.

The *interrogative* text, on the other hand, disrupts the unity of the reader by discouraging identification with a unified subject of the enunciation. The position of the 'author' inscribed in the text, if it can be located at all, is seen as questioning or as contradictory. Thus, even if the interrogative text does not precisely, in Benveniste's terms, seek 'to obtain some information' from the reader, it does literally invite the reader to produce answers to the questions it implicitly or explicitly raises.

These three categories, of course, are in no sense self-contained and mutually exclusive, nor are their characteristics timelessly sealed within specific texts. It is possible to locate elements of one modality in a text characterized predominantly by another. More important, a different way of reading, a different critical approach can transfer a text from one modality to another. None the less, Benveniste's classification may perhaps provide a way of isolating certain distinguishing formal features of what I have called the interrogative text.

I have defined classic realism as that form which is characterized by illusionism, narrative leading to closure, and a hierarchy of voices (pp. 64–5 above). The imperative text is not usually fictional, since it is marked as referring to the world outside the text; it therefore displays neither illusionism nor narrative leading to closure. The interrogative text, on the other hand, may well be fictional, but the narrative does not lead to that form of closure which in classic realism is also disclosure. As Althusser says of Brecht, 'he wanted to make the spectator into an actor who would complete the unfinished play . . .' (Althusser

1969: 146). The interrogative text invites an answer or answers to the questions it poses. Further, if the interrogative text is illusionist, it also tends to employ devices to undermine the illusion, to draw attention to its own textuality. The reader is distanced, at least from time to time, rather than wholly interpolated into a fictional world. Above all, the interrogative text differs from the classic realist text in the absence of a single privileged narrative which contains and places all the others.

The world represented in the interrogative text includes what Althusser calls 'an internal distance' from the ideology in which it is held, which permits the reader to construct from within the text a critique of this ideology (Althusser 1971: 204). In other words, the interrogative text refuses a single point of view, however complex and comprehensive, but brings points of view into unresolved collision or contradiction. It therefore refuses the hierarchy of voices of classic realism, and no authorial or authoritative voice points to a single position which is the place of the coherence of meaning.[1] In John Berger's story about a girl who goes to the doctor in tears because, as it finally emerges, her drudgery at the local laundry is intolerable, the concluding sentences call in question any generalized optimism engendered by the doctor's promise of decisive action on her behalf:

> Through the surgery window he saw her walking up the lane to the common, to the house in which he had delivered her sixteen years ago. After she had turned the corner, he continued to stare at the stone walls on either side of the lane. Once they were dry walls. Now their stones were cemented together.
>
> (Berger and Mohr 1976: 33)

The image of the cemented stones, naturalistically motivated but also open to metaphorical reading, suggests that stability which results from the smoothing over of differences in modern society. The reader is invited to reflect on the relationship between the fixity of this concluding *image* and the dynamic conclusion of the *story*, the doctor's alleviation of social distress in a single instance.

To take a much earlier example, from a period when the social relations generated by the capitalist mode of production were not so firmly established, and therefore perhaps not so readily taken for granted as 'natural', in *Moll Flanders* contradiction is a structural principle of the text. Within Moll's account of her own life it is apparent that sentiment (sexual or maternal) repeatedly gives way to calculation in the interests of survival, and the socially approved desire for independence ('to be a lady') generates crime, until finally it is penitence which leads to prosperity. The recurrent attempts of critics to establish irony in the narrative, in order to attribute a coherent and unified position to Defoe, are above all a way of evading confrontation with the social and ideological contradictions of capitalism as they are foregrounded in the text.

Swift, who, as Gabriel Josipovici recognizes, has more in common with modernism than with classic realism, offers a further example of the absence of a clear authorial and thus authoritative point of view. Terry Eagleton describes the fourth book of *Gulliver's Travels* in the following terms:

> Gulliver despises men as Yahoos and identifies with the Houyhnhnms; the Houyhnhnms despise the Yahoos and regard Gulliver as one of them; we are amused by the Houyhnhnms and by Gulliver's delusions, but are close enough to the Yahoos for the amusement to be uneasy; and to cap it all there are some respects in which the Yahoos *are* superior to men. There is no way for the reader to 'totalise' these contradictions, which the text so adroitly springs upon him; he is merely caught in their dialectical interplay, rendered as eccentric to himself as the lunatic Gulliver, unable to turn to the refuge of an assuring authorial voice.
>
> (Eagleton 1977: 58)

The consistently interrogative writer who comes most readily to mind is, of course, Brecht, who anticipated so much of this theory. *Galileo*, for instance, dramatizes the contradiction between ideology and knowledge and poses the question how to behave rightly in an authoritarian society. Galileo recants and sets back the Enlightenment in Europe; but he completes the *Discorsi*. His followers are shocked by his lack of heroism. The spectator is alternately in sympathy with and repelled by the behaviour of Galileo himself, identifying with his predicament and his thirst for knowledge, and rejecting his contemptuous treatment of other people. 'Brecht' can be located in the obvious sense that the text sympathizes with the revolutionary science of Galileo as against the authority of the Church, but no answer is given to the central question posed by the text. In conjunction with Brecht's formal alienation effects, this has the consequence of enlisting the spectator in the questioning process. He or she is alternately interpolated, drawn in to the events, and distanced, pulled out of the fixity of ideology and into active critical debate.

The Renaissance setting of *Galileo* is partly a characteristically Brechtian distancing device, which both removes the problem from the heat of current contentions and allows its modern relevance to become apparent. To the extent, however, that the play refers to history, it again points to the collision of ideologies within the Renaissance. A recognition of political contradiction is also recurrent in the literature of the period. Marlowe's *Tamburlaine the Great*, played half a century before the Civil War, has themes and imagery in common with Marvell's 'Horatian Ode' to Cromwell, written after the death of Charles 1. Both present in colliding images of magnificence and horror, heroism and brutality, revolutionary leaders who rise from the people and maintain their power by divine providence and by violence.

Tamburlaine's most heroic and most famous speech which, in spite of a certain ironic undercurrent of allusions to the Fall, sounds on the surface like the apotheosis of Renaissance humanism, is proclaimed over the body of the dying Cosroe, one of the first of Tamburlaine's victims in the play (I Tamburlaine, II, vii). The contradiction between the high sentiment of the speech and the visual spectacle of Cosroe's dying agonies anticipates the series of contrasts and contradictions which is to follow. Much of Tamburlaine's violence is displayed on the stage, and the audience is invited to consider the implications of the juxtaposition of visual brutality and 'high astounding terms'. To 'ride in triumph through Persepolis' (II, v, 50) is also to practise a remorseless and apparently endless tyranny.

In Marvell's version, Cromwell is compared to lightning, rending palaces and temples, kings and nations, on behalf of 'angry heaven'. And the poem chillingly concludes, 'The same arts that did gain/A power, must it maintain'. To identify an immature Marlowe with

Tamburlaine's aspirations, or to smooth over the contradictions in the 'Horatian Ode' by attributing to Marvell a non-contradictory ideology of Loyalism is to refuse to enter into the debates about revolution, authority and tyranny initiated in the texts.

Shakespeare's specifically political plays tend to be constructed on a similar basis of contrasts and collisions. We may think, for instance, of the history plays, which draw attention to 'the contradiction between the sacredness of the crown and the individual called upon by birth to wear it, who might be noble and worthy or selfish, weak and surrounded with bad counsellors' (Heinemann 1977: 14). A structural feature of the *Henry IV* plays is the juxtaposition of Hotspur's heroic mode of address and Falstaff's pragmatic one: each has an energy and a vitality which prevents the audience from simply dismissing one of the conflicting points of view; each at the same time is presented to some degree ironically.

In *Julius Caesar* political contradiction is rendered emblematic in Brutus's speech immediately after the assassination of Caesar. Brutus calls on the conspirators to present at once an image of violence and a cry of peace:

> Stoop, Romans, stoop,
> And let us bathe our hands in Caesar's blood
> Up to the elbows, and besmear our swords.
> Then walk we forth, even to the market-place,
> And waving our red weapons o'er our heads,
> Let's all cry 'Peace, freedom and liberty!'

(III, i, 106–11)

Like Brecht's *Galileo*, *Julius Caesar* is set in a remote past which has obvious relevance to the present, and like *Galileo* it invites the audience to ponder the problems of freedom and authority, individual integrity and social liberation, honest action in a dishonest world. If Brutus's quest for peace through violence is mistaken, the cause is not simply a personal ethical error.

Coriolanus dramatizes the contradictory truth that heroic individualism is both necessary to and destructive of a militaristic society. Here, as in *Galileo*, the audience is discouraged from identification with the protagonist. No single voice is privileged: the opposing groups, poles of the action, patricians and people, are both in a state of internal conflict. The self-seeking tribunes, appointed as a concession to the people, simply mislead them; the organic and hierarchic ideology of Menenius collides with the militaristic individualism of Coriolanus. No single figure within the text possesses a full grasp of the 'truth'; none is in control of the action. At the same time, no invisible narration situates the others by means of readily identifiable irony. As a result, the only position of intelligibility offered to the spectator by the play in its entirety is an actively critical one.

It is not, perhaps, irrelevant that the Elizabethan theatre is itself in process, in a state of transition between the patently non-illusionist and emblematic medieval stage and the proscenium theatres of the Restoration period. The frame provided by the proscenium arch, and the containment of the action within the framed stage, offers a single, unified point of view for the audience, a comprehensive vision of the events dramatized, which is also a comprehending and therefore authoritative vision, and this is thus the theatrical form appropriate to classic realism. In this context it is worth remembering that the codes of perspective in painting also have their origin in the Renaissance, and perspective too makes possible a mode of representation in which the fictional world is presented to the perceiving eye of the spectator as a unified spectacle to be known, understood, dominated. 'Eye and knowledge come together; subject, object and the distance of the steady observation that allows the one to master the other. . . .' (Heath 1976: 77). The Elizabethan stage, on the other hand, is more open, and the relationship between players and audience less controlled and predictable. Minimal scenery and blank verse pull against illusionism at the same time as the enriching of the language of drama in comparison to the medieval theatre deepens audience involvement in the fictional world of the play. The concept of a self-contained fictional world barely exists before the introduction of the raised stage in the mid-sixteenth century, and direct address to the audience remains common in the Elizabethan theatre. The transitional nature of the Renaissance theatre facilitates the dialectical relationship between identification and distance which enlists the audience in contradiction.

But the interrogative text in this period is not confined to the stage, nor are its themes inevitably political. Marvell often uses the dialogue form in his poems to set up the terms of a debate which is not completed within the text. In 'A Dialogue between Soul and Body', for instance, it is the Body which, startlingly, has the last word, but there is no sense that the debate is over as the poem ends, and it is the expectation of closure generated by classic realism, I suggest, which has led to the critical conjecture, on purely formal grounds, that the poem is incomplete. Donne's 'Death be not Proud' dramatizes the speaker's fear of death in its imagery and syntax even while asserting death's powerlessness. In 'The Sun Rising' Donne brings love and time into collision in such a way that the confident assertion of the transcendence of love is constantly undermined by the intrusion of a substantial world of time on the one hand and patently false logic in support of love's timelessness on the other. It is not a simple question of dramatic irony, a monologue spoken by a deluded lover: the contradictions in the poem cannot be resolved by reference to a knowing and non-contradictory subject of the enunciation. In Marvell's poem the utterances of soul and body are isolated from each other in a formal debate. There is no logical victory for either side, and no intervention by the 'author' to resolve the debate. In Donne's poems the contrary positions are an ironic presence which put in question but do not overturn the central arguments. As a result, the reader is placed in the contradictory position of believing what is shown to be unbelievable. In consequence, Christian dualism, Christian faith and profane love are displaced from the category of timeless and universal human experience and glimpsed momentarily as unstable textual configurations whose contradictions cannot be resolved within the specific culture which is the condition of their existence.

One final theatrical example from the Renaissance in an attempt to summarize the formal characteristics of the interrogative text. *The Winter's Tale*, like *What Maisie Knew*, is about degrees of 'knowing', but unlike *What Maisie Knew* it finally refuses the audience the reassurance of a position of knowledge shared with the subjects of the *énoncé* and the enunciation. The play falls fairly clearly into two parts, divided by a chronological gap of sixteen years and a formal gap between tragicomedy and romance.[2] The first part of the play bears some resemblance to classic realism: its mode is narrative, and as illusionist as is consistent with the theatre of the period, and the audience is put in a position of knowledge which is confirmed within the text by the authoritative pronouncement of the oracle: 'Hermione is chaste; Polixenes blameless; Camillo a true subject; Leontes a jealous tyrant . . .' (III, ii, 130–1). This is what we had supposed. The disturbing element for a classic realist reading of the first part of the play is the totally unpredicted and unmotivated onset of the jealousy of Leontes immediately following his affirmation in the strongest terms of the value of his marriage. The unified subjectivity of, say, Othello, is here totally absent: Leontes is not misled gradually by false evidence; he is, simply, instantly and arbitrarily transformed. Nor is the jealousy presented as a coherent element in a consistent character: he is not shown as irrational or tyrannical in any other sphere.

None the less, in the collision between the certainty of Leontes and the knowledge of all the other characters there is no contradiction for the audience: in Acts I–III Leontes is clearly deluded. Act IV goes on to make ironic play with the hierarchy of degrees of knowledge. The knowing voice of Autolycus is more sophisticated than the innocent exchanges of the shepherds, but the audience is put in a position to penetrate his disguises as it also penetrates those of Polixenes and Camillo. Dramatic ironies here offer the spectator a position of knowledge. Perdita is a princess who believes herself to be a shepherdess playing a goddess, and the audience savours the irony of the many allusions to her as metaphorically a queen or a princess by characters who know less than we do. Perdita 'knows' that she will never marry Florizel ('I told you what would come of this . . . this dream of mine/Being now awake, I'll queen it no inch farther', IV, iv, 439–41), but the audience knows, on the authority of the oracle as well as the codes of romance, that her true identity will be revealed.

But in Act V, in the moment of closure, the play unexpectedly turns on the audience and puts in question *its* knowledge, as the statue of Hermione comes to life. The statue scene is in a sense gratuitous. Not only is it quite contrary to the closure of the source story, *Pandosto*, but in the play itself no allusion to Hermione's resurrection is made by the oracle, which has been the reliable source of the audience's knowledge to this point. The text provides enough hints of a 'realist' explanation of Hermione's return to life to make such a reading possible (e.g. V, ii, 103), but to believe that Hermione has remained in hiding for sixteen years makes a cruel parody of the mourning of Leontes and an absurdity of Paulina's solemn invocation to the statue, and is thus unsatisfactory precisely at the 'realist' level. No explanation is given to the audience, which simply confronts the apparent contradiction of Hermione's 'I . . . have preserved/Myself' (V, iii, 125–8) and Leontes's 'I saw her,/As I thought, dead' (V, iii, 139–40).

On either reading the play abandons plausibility, 'truth'. The statue scene is incompatible with classic realism not simply because it is improbable but because it is not explained, not related in intelligible ways to the events or characters of the text. Thus its effect is quite distinct from that of the improbable coincidences of the romance episodes. It breaks with classic realism as they do not.

Paulina presents Hermione's resurrection in the language of mystery, magic, and above all, art. It is a spectacle, but one which for the characters in the play literally comes alive, as illusionism may be said to come alive for the audience. But to give the metaphor literal significance in this way is to defamiliarize it, to isolate it for contemplation. If fiction can bring to life *without explanation* characters it has killed, disrupt intelligible patterns of relationship between events, then surely it refuses the responsibility of art to confront real issues?

> That she is living,
> Were it but told you, should be hooted at
> Like an old tale; but appears she lives.

> (V, iii, 115–17)

The scene, as close to illusionism as any part of Shakespeare in terms of the vocabulary and the speech rhythms of the verse, draws attention to its own implausibility by a contemptuous reference to fiction which has the effect of challenging the illusion.

The Winter's Tale abounds in references to fiction, and to the relationship between fiction and truth:

Mopsa. I love a ballad in print a-life, for then we are sure they are true.
Aut. Here's one to a very doleful tune: how a usurer's wife was brought

> to bed of twenty money-bags at a burden, and how she long'd to
> eat adders' heads and toads carbonado'd.
>
> *Mopsa.* It is true, think you?
>
> *Aut.* Very true, and but a month old.
>
> *Dorcas.* Bless me from marrying a usurer!
>
> *Aut.* Here's the midwife's name to it, one Mistress Taleporter, and five
> or six honest wives that were present. Why should I carry lies
> abroad?
>
> *Mopsa.* Pray you now, buy it.
>
> (IV, iv, 256–66)

The shepherds are naive and therefore comic, but their premises are
not necessarily unsound. At court, too, truth to nature is the criterion
of success in the work of 'that rare Italian master, Julio Romano,
who, had he himself eternity and could put breath into his work,
would beguile nature of her custom, so perfectly he is her ape' (V, ii,
93–6).

Meanwhile, the text itself is increasingly dismissive of its own pre-
tensions to truth. Its title signifies an old wives' tale. Mamillius's promise of a tale of sprites and goblins is immediately followed by the entry
of Leontes to imprison Hermione, as if in ironic completion of the
child's story. In Act V the text three times compares what it recounts to
an old tale. It also suggests that the events it records are worthy of the
ballad-makers, and the allusion refers us straight back to the absurd
fantasies of Autolycus's merchandize, pointing to the incredibility of
what the audience is being invited to believe.

The Winter's Tale, then, both juxtaposes and embodies contradictory
notions of the relationship between fiction and truth. The first part of
the play imparts to the audience a clear 'knowledge' of the dangers of
subjectivity as a source of knowledge; the second part withholds the
'knowledge' which would make the play's action fully intelligible and
thus puts in question for the audience what it is to know *in* fiction and
through fiction. The play seems in most respects to begin as a representation of the world outside fiction and to uphold the concept of
art as a form of truth. But the second part of the play, while drawing
explicit attention to this concept, distances itself from it and finally
redefines itself as text, refusing to issue a guarantee of its own truth.

In this way it challenges the realist concept of art, and invites the spectators to reflect on fiction as a discursive practice and the ways in which textuality allows them to grasp their relation to the real relations in which they live.

6

THE WORK OF READING

BARTHES AND MACHEREY

There is always a danger that a radical literary criticism will simply create a new canon of acceptable texts, merely reversing old value judgements, rather than questioning their fundamental assumptions, as did, for instance, New Criticism (see Chapter 2). In arguing that the interrogative text enlists the reader in contradiction, while classic realism does its best to efface contradiction, I do not mean to suggest that the interrogative text is therefore 'good' and classic realism ideological, misleading and therefore 'bad'. But if we are not simply to subject ourselves (in every sense) to ideology, we need a new way of approaching classic realism.

In the early stages of its development in France semiology (semiotics) concerned itself above all with the unmasking of ideology masquerading as truth. Barthes's *Mythologies* (1957, English translation 1972) is the classic exposition of the ways in which ideology is naturalized in the usages, images and myths of contemporary society. But literary realism was too valuable, and perhaps too powerful, to be handed to the ruling class without a struggle. It was apparent that it was no longer possible to regard the classic realist text as a reflection of the world. As an alternative, it was possible to recognize it as a *construct* and so to treat it as available for analysis of the process and conditions of its construction out of the available textual materials. Ideology, masquerading as coherence and plenitude, is in practice inconsistent, limited, contradictory, and the realist text, as a crystallization of ideology, participates in this incompleteness, even while it diverts attention from the fact in the apparent plenitude of narrative closure. The object of this analysis is to examine the *process of its production* – not the private experience of the individual author, but the mode of production, the materials and their arrangement in the work. The aim is to locate the point of contradiction within the text, the point at which it transgresses the limits within which it is constructed, breaks free of the constraints imposed by its own realist form. Composed of contradictions, the text is no longer restricted to a single, harmonious and authoritative reading. Instead it becomes *plural*, open to rereading, no longer an object for passive consumption but an object of work by the reader to produce meaning.

Again the classic exposition is by Roland Barthes. In S/Z, first published in 1970 (English translation 1975), Barthes analyses a short story by Balzac. *Sarrasine* is a classic realist text concerning a castrato singer and a fortune. The narrative turns on a series of enigmas (what is the source of the fortune? who is the little old man? who is La Zambinella? what is the connection between all three?).

Even in summarizing the story in this way it is necessary to 'lie': there are not 'three' but two, since the little old 'man' is 'La' Zambinella. Barthes breaks the text into fragments of varying lengths for analysis, and adds a number of 'divagations', pieces of more generalized commentary and exploration, to show *Sarrasine* as a 'limit-text', a text which uses the modes of classic realism in ways which constitute a series of 'transgressions' of classic realism itself. The sense of plenitude, of a full understanding of a coherent text which is the normal result of reading the realist narrative, cannot here be achieved. It is not only that castration cannot be named in a text of this period. The text is compelled to transgress the conventional antithesis between the genders whenever it uses a pronoun to speak of the castrato. The story concerns the scandal of castration and the death of desire which follows its revelation; it concerns the scandalous origin of wealth; and it demonstrates the collapse of language, of antithesis (difference) as a source of meaning, which is involved in the disclosure of these scandals.

Each of these elements of the text provides a point of entry into it, none privileged, and these approaches constitute the degree of polyphony, the 'parsimonious plural' of the readable (lisible) text. The classic realist text moves inevitably and irreversibly to an end, to the conclusion of an ordered series of events, to the disclosure of what has been concealed. But even in the realist text certain modes of significa-tion within the discourse – the symbolic, the codes of reference and the semes – evade the constraints of the narrative sequence. To the extent that these are 'reversible', free-floating and of indeterminate authority, the text is plural. In the writable (scriptible), wholly plural text all statements are of indeterminate origin, no single voice is privileged, and no consistent and coherent plot constrains the free play of the voices. The totally writable, plural text does not exist. At the opposite extreme, the readable text is barely plural. The readable text is mer-chandize to be consumed, while the plural text requires the production of meanings through the identification of its polyphony. Reading in order to produce the text as a newly intelligible, plural object is the work of criticism.

Barthes's own mode of writing demonstrates his contempt for the readable: S/Z is itself a polyphonic critical text. It is impossible to summarize adequately, to reduce to systematic accessibility, and it is noticeable that the book contains no totalizing conclusion. Like Sarrasine, S/Z offers a number of points of entry, critical observations which generate trains of thought in the reader, but it would be contrary to Barthes's own (anarchist) argument to order all these into a single, coherent methodology, to constitute a new, unitary way of reading, however comprehensive, and so to become the (authoritative) author of a new critical orthodoxy. As a result, the experience of reading S/Z is at once frustrating and exhilarating. Though it offers a model in one sense – S/Z implies a new kind of critical practice – it would almost certainly not be possible (or useful) to attempt a wholesale imitation of its critical method(s).

It seems clear that one of the most influential precursors of S/Z, though Barthes does not allude to it, was Pierre Macherey's (Marxist) A Theory of Literary Production, first published in 1966 (English translation 1978). Despite real and important differences between them, there are similarities worth noting. For instance, Macherey anticipates Barthes in demonstrating that contradiction is a condition of narrative. The classic realist text is constructed on the basis of enigma. Information is initially withheld on condition of a 'promise' to the reader that it will finally be revealed. The disclosure of this 'truth' brings the story to an end. The movement of narrative is thus both towards disclosure – the end of the story – and towards concealment – prolonging itself by delaying the end of the story through a series of 'reticences', as Barthes calls them, snares for the reader, partial answers to the questions raised, equivocations (Macherey 1978: 28–9; Barthes 1975: 75–6).

Further, narrative involves the reader in an experience of the inevitable in the form of the unforeseen (Macherey 1978: 43). The hero encounters an obstacle: will he attempt to overcome it or abandon the quest? The answer is already determined, though the reader, who has only to turn the page to discover it, experiences the moment as one of choice for the hero. In fact, of course, if the narrative is to continue the hero must go on (Barthes 1975: 135). Thus the author's autonomy is to some degree illusory. In one sense the author determines the nature of the story: he or she decides what happens. In another sense, however, this decision is itself determined by the constraints of the narrative (Macherey 1978: 48), or by what Barthes calls the *interest* (in both the psychological and the economic senses) of the story (Barthes 1975: 135).

The formal constraints imposed by literary form on the project of the work in the process of literary production constitute the structural principle of Macherey's analysis. It is a mistake to reduce the text to the product of a single cause, authorial determination or the mechanics of the narrative. On the contrary, the literary work 'is composed from a real diversity of elements which give it substance' (Macherey 1978: 49). There may be a direct contradiction between the project and the formal constraints, and in the transgression thus created it is possible to locate an important object of the critical quest.

Fiction for Macherey (he deals mainly with classic realist narrative), is intimately related to ideology, but the two are not identical. Literature is a specific and irreducible form of textuality, but the language which constitutes the raw material of the text is the language of ideology. It is thus an inadequate language, incomplete, partial, incapable of concealing the real contradictions it is its purpose to efface.

This language, normally in flux, is arrested, 'congealed' by the literary text.

The realist text is a determinate representation, an intelligible structure which claims to convey intelligible relationships between its elements. In its attempt to create a coherent and internally consistent fictive world the text, in spite of itself, exposes incoherences, omissions, absences and transgressions which in turn reveal the inability of the language of ideology to create coherence. This becomes apparent because the contradiction between the diverse elements drawn from different discourses, the ideological project and the literary form, creates an absence at the centre of the work.[1] The text is divided, split as the Lacanian subject is split, and Macherey compares the 'lack' in the consciousness of the work, its silence, what it cannot say, with the unconscious which Freud explored (85).

The unconscious of the work (not, it must be insisted, of the author) is constructed in the moment of its entry into literary form, in the gap between the ideological project and the specifically literary text. Thus the text is no more a transcendent unity than the human subject. The novels of Jules Verne, for instance, whose work Macherey analyses in some detail, indicate that 'if Jules Verne chose to be the spokesman of a certain ideological condition, he could not choose to be what he in fact became' (94).

What Macherey reveals in Verne's *The Secret of the Island* is an unpredicted and contradictory element, disrupting the colonialist ideology which informs the conscious project of the work. Within the narrative, which concerns the willing surrender of nature to improvement by a team of civilized and civilizing colonizers, there insists an older and contrary myth which the consciousness of the text rejects. Unexplained events imply another mysterious influence on what is apparently a desert island. Captain Nemo's secret presence, and his effect on the fate of the castaways from a subterranean cave, is the source of the series of enigmas and the final disclosure which constitute the narrative. But his existence in the text has no part in the overt ideological project. On the contrary, it represents the return of the repressed in the form of a re-enacting of the myth of Robinson Crusoe. This myth evokes both a literary ancestor – Defoe's story – on which all subsequent castaway stories are to some degree conditional, and an ancestral relationship to nature – the creation of an economy by Crusoe's solitary struggle to appropriate and transform the island – on which subsequent bourgeois society is also conditional.

The Robinson Crusoe story, the antithesis of the conscious project of the narrative, is also the condition of its existence. It returns, as the repressed experience returns to the consciousness of the patient in dreams and slips of the tongue, and in doing so it unconsciously draws attention to an origin and a history from which both desert island stories and triumphant bourgeois ideology are unable to cut themselves off, and with which they must settle their account. *The Secret of the Island* thus reveals, through the discord within it between the conscious project and the insistence of the disruptive unconscious, the limits of the coherence of nineteenth-century ideology.

The object of the critic, then, is to seek not the unity of the work, but the multiplicity and diversity of its possible meanings, its incompleteness, the omissions which it displays but cannot describe, and above all its contradictions. In its absences, and in the collisions between its divergent meanings, the text implicitly criticizes its own ideology; it contains within itself the critique of its own values, in the sense that it is available for a new process of production of meaning by the reader, and in this process it can provide a real knowledge of the limits of ideological representation.

Macherey's way of reading is precisely contrary to traditional Anglo-American critical practice, where the quest is for the unity of the work, its coherence, a way of repairing any deficiencies in consistency by reference to the author's philosophy or the contemporary world picture. In thus smoothing out contradiction, closing the text, criticism becomes the accomplice of ideology. Having created a canon of acceptable texts, criticism then provides them with acceptable interpretations, thus effectively censoring any elements in them which come into collision with the dominant ideology. The project of reading as work, on the other hand, is to open the text, to release the possible positions of its intelligibility, including those which reveal the partiality (in both senses) of the ideology inscribed in the text.

Such a way of reading would ultimately have the consequence of redrawing the map of 'Eng. Lit.'. In order to explore the usefulness of extending the existing canon, and at the same time of analysing other forms besides realist fiction in this way, I propose to consider aspects first of the Sherlock Holmes stories and then of Matthew Arnold's 'The Scholar-Gipsy'.[2]

SHERLOCK HOLMES

In locating the transitions and uncertainties of the text it is important to remember, Macherey insists, sustaining the parallel with psycho-analysis, that the problem of the work is not the same as its *consciousness* of a problem (Macherey 1978: 93). In 'Charles Augustus Milverton', one of the short stories from *The Return of Sherlock Holmes*, Conan Doyle presents the reader with an ethical problem. Milverton is a blackmailer; blackmail is a crime not easily brought to justice, since the victims are inevitably unwilling to make the matter public; the text therefore proposes for the reader's consideration that in such a case illegal action may be ethical. Holmes plans to burgle Milverton's house to recover the letters which are at stake, and both Watson and the text appear to conclude, after due consideration, that the action is morally justifiable. The structure of the narrative is symmetrical: one victim initiates the plot, another concludes it. While Holmes and Watson hide in Milverton's study, a woman shoots him, protesting that he has ruined her life. Inspector Lestrade asks Holmes to help catch the murderer. Holmes replies that certain crimes justify private revenge, that his sympathies are with the criminal and that he will not handle the case. The reader is left to ponder the ethical implications of his position.

Meanwhile, on the fringes of the text, another narrative is sketched. It too contains problems but these are not foregrounded. Holmes's client is the Lady Eva Blackwell, a beautiful debutante who is to be married to the Earl of Dovercourt. Milverton has secured letters she has written 'to an impecunious young squire in the country'. Lady Eva does not appear in the narrative in person. The content of the letters is not specified, but they are 'imprudent, Watson, nothing worse'. Milverton describes them as 'sprightly'. Holmes's sympathies, and ours, are with the Lady Eva. None the less we, and Holmes, accept without question on the one hand that the marriage with the Earl of Dovercourt is a desirable one and, on the other, that were he to see the letters, he would certainly break off the match. The text's elusiveness on the content of the letters, and the absence of the Lady Eva herself, deflects the reader's attention from the potentially contradictory ideology of marriage which the narrative takes for granted.

This second narrative is also symmetrical. The murderer too is a woman with a past. She is not identified. Milverton has sent her letters to her husband, who in consequence 'broke his gallant heart and died'. Again the text is unable to be precise about the content of the letters, since to do so would be to risk losing the sympathy of the reader for either the woman or her husband.

In the mean time Holmes has become engaged. By offering to marry Milverton's housemaid he has secured information about the lay-out of the house he is to burgle. Watson remonstrates about the subsequent fate of the girl, but Holmes replies:

> You can't help it, my dear Watson. You must play your cards as best you can when such a stake is on the table. However, I rejoice to say that I have a hated rival who will certainly cut me out the instant that my back is turned. What a splendid night it is.

The housemaid is not further discussed in the story.

The sexuality of these three shadowy women motivates the narrative and yet is barely present in it. The disclosure which ends the story is thus scarcely a disclosure at all. Symbolically Holmes has burnt the letters, records of women's sexuality. Watson's opening paragraph constitutes an apology for the 'reticence' of the narrative: '. . . with *due suppression* the story may be told . . .'; 'The reader will excuse me if I conceal the date *or any other fact* . . .' (my italics).

The project of the Sherlock Holmes stories is to dispel magic and mystery, to make everything explicit, accountable, subject to scientific analysis. The phrase most familiar to all readers – 'Elementary, my dear Watson' – is in fact a misquotation, but its familiarity is no accident since it precisely captures the central concern of the stories. Holmes and Watson are both men of science. Holmes, the 'genius', is a scientific conjuror who insists on disclosing how the trick is done. The stories begin in enigma, mystery, the impossible, and conclude with an explanation which makes it clear that logical deduction and scientific method render all mysteries accountable to reason:

I am afraid that my explanation may disillusionize you, but it has always been my habit to hide none of my methods, either from my friend Watson or from anyone who might take an intelligent interest in them.

('The Reigate Squires', *The Memoirs of Sherlock Holmes*)

The stories are a plea for science not only in the spheres conventionally associated with detection (footprints, traces of hair or cloth, cigarette ends), where they have been deservedly influential on forensic practice, but in all areas. They reflect the widespread optimism characteristic of their period concerning the comprehensive power of positivist science. Holmes's ability to deduce Watson's train of thought, for instance, is repeatedly displayed, and it owes nothing to the supernatural. Once explained, the reasoning process always appears 'absurdly simple', open to the commonest of common sense.

The project of the stories themselves, enigma followed by disclosure, echoes precisely the structure of the classic realist text. The narrator himself draws attention to the parallel between them:

'Excellent!' I cried.

'Elementary,' said he. 'It is one of those instances where the reasoner can produce an effect which seems remarkable to his neighbour because the latter has missed the one little point which is the basis of the deduction. The same may be said, my dear fellow, for the effect of some of these little sketches of yours, which is entirely meretricious, depending as it does upon your retaining in your own hands some factors in the problem which are never imparted to the reader. Now, at present I am in the position of these same readers, for I hold in this hand several threads of one of the strangest cases which ever perplexed a man's brain, and yet I lack the one or two which are needful to complete my theory. But I'll have them, Watson, I'll have them!'

('The Crooked Man', *Memoirs*)

(The passage is quoted by Macherey in his discussion of the characteristic structure of narrative, 1978: 35.)

The project also requires the maximum degree of 'realism' – verisimilitude, plausibility. In the interest of science no hint of the fantastic or the implausible is permitted to remain once the disclosure is complete. This is why even their own existence as writing is so frequently discussed within the texts. The stories are alluded to as Watson's 'little sketches', his 'memoirs'. They resemble fictions because of Watson's unscientific weakness for story-telling:

> I must admit, Watson, that you have some power of selection which atones for much which I deplore in your narratives. Your fatal habit of looking at everything from the point of view of a story instead of as a scientific exercise has ruined what might have been an instructive and even classical series of demonstrations.
>
> ('The Abbey Grange', *Return*)

In other words, the fiction itself accounts even for its own fictionality, and the text thus appears wholly transparent. The success with which the Sherlock Holmes stories achieve an illusion of reality is repeatedly demonstrated. In their foreword to The *Sherlock Holmes Companion* (1962) Michael and Mollie Hardwick comment on their own recurrent illusion 'that we were dealing with a figure of real life rather than of fiction. How vital Holmes appears, compared with many people of one's own acquaintance.'

De Waal's bibliography of Sherlock Holmes lists 25 'Sherlockian' periodicals apparently largely devoted to conjectures, based on the 'evidence' of the stories, concerning matters only hinted at in the texts – Holmes's education, his income and his romantic and sexual adventures. According to the *Times* in December 1967, letters to Sherlock Holmes were then still commonly addressed to 221B Baker Street, many of them asking for the detective's help.

None the less these stories, whose overt project is total explicitness, total verisimilitude in the interests of a plea for scientificity, are haunted by shadowy, mysterious and often silent women. Their silence repeatedly conceals their sexuality, investing it with a dark and magical quality which is beyond the reach of scientific knowledge. In 'The Greek Interpreter' (*Memoirs*) Sophie Kratides has run away with a man. Though she is the pivot of the plot, she appears only briefly: 'I could not see her clearly enough to know more than that she was tall and graceful, with black hair, and clad in some sort of loose white gown.'

Connotatively the white gown marks her as still virginal and her flight as the result of romance rather than desire. At the same time the dim light surrounds her with shadow, the unknown. 'The Crooked Man' concerns Mrs Barclay, whose husband is found dead on the day of her meeting with her lover of many years before. Mrs Barclay is now insensible, 'temporarily insane' since the night of the murder and therefore unable to speak. In 'The Dancing Men' (Return) Mrs Elsie Cubitt, once engaged to a criminal, longs to speak but cannot bring herself to break her silence. By the time Holmes arrives she is unconscious, and she remains so for the rest of the story. Ironically the narrative concerns the breaking of the code which enables her former lover to communicate with her. Elsie's only contribution to the correspondence is the word, 'Never'. The precise nature of their relationship is left mysterious, constructed of contrary suggestions. Holmes says she feared and hated him; the lover claims, 'She had been engaged to me, and she would have married me, I believe, if I had taken over another profession.' When her husband moves to shoot the man whose coded messages are the source of a 'terror' which is 'wearing her away', Elsie restrains him with compulsive strength. On the question of her motives the text is characteristically elusive. Her husband recounts the story:

> I was angry with my wife that night for having held me back when I might have caught the skulking rascal. She said that she feared that I might come to harm. For an instant it had crossed my mind that what she really feared was that *he* might come to harm, for I could not doubt that she knew who this man was and what he meant by those strange signals. But there is a tone in my wife's voice, Mr Holmes, and a look in her eyes which forbid doubt, and I am sure that it was indeed my own safety that was in her mind.

After her husband's death Elsie remains a widow, faithful to his memory and devoting her life to the care of the poor, apparently expiating something unspecified, perhaps an act or a state of feeling, remote or recent.

'The Dancing Men' is 'about' Holmes's method of breaking the cipher. Its project is to dispel any magic from the deciphering process.

Elsie's silence is in the interest of the story since she knows the code. But she also 'knows' her feelings towards her former lover. Contained in the completed and fully disclosed story of the decipherment is another uncompleted and undisclosed narrative which is more than merely peripheral to the text as a whole. Elsie's past is central and causal. As a result, the text with its project of dispelling mystery is haunted by the mysterious state of mind of a woman who is unable to speak.

The classic realist text had not yet developed a way of signifying women's sexuality except in a metaphoric or symbolic mode whose presence disrupts the realist surface. Joyce and Lawrence were beginning to experiment at this time with modes of sexual signification but in order to do so they largely abandoned the codes of realism. So much is readily apparent. What is more significant, however, is that the presentation of so many women in the Sherlock Holmes stories as shadowy, mysterious and magical figures precisely contradicts the project of explicitness, transgresses the values of the texts, and in doing so throws into relief the poverty of the contemporary concept of science. These stories, pleas for a total explicitness about the world, are unable to explain an area which none the less they cannot ignore. The version of science which the texts present would constitute a clear challenge to ideology: the interpretation of all areas of life, physical, social and psychological, is to be subject to rational scrutiny and the requirements of coherent theorization. Confronted, however, by an area in which ideology itself is uncertain, the Sherlock Holmes stories display the limits of their own project and are compelled to manifest the inadequacy of a bourgeois scientificity which, working within the constraints of ideology, is thus unable to challenge it.

Perhaps the most interesting case, since it introduces an additional area of shadow, is 'The Second Stain' (Return), which concerns two letters. Lady Hilda Trelawney Hope does speak. She has written before her marriage 'an indiscreet letter . . . a foolish letter, a letter of an impulsive, loving girl.' Had her husband read the letter, his confidence in her would have been for ever destroyed. Her husband is nevertheless presented as entirely sympathetic, and here again we encounter the familiar contradiction between a husband's supposed reaction, accepted as just, and the reaction offered to the reader by the text. In return for her original letter Lady Hilda gives her blackmailer a letter from 'a certain foreign potentate', stolen from the dispatch box of her husband, the European Secretary of State. This political letter is symbolically parallel to the first sexual one. Its contents are equally elusive but it too is 'indiscreet', 'hot-headed'; certain phrases in it are 'provocative'. Its publication would produce 'a most dangerous state of feeling' in the nation. Lady Hilda's innocent folly is the cause of the theft: she knows nothing of politics and was not in a position to understand the consequences of her action. Holmes ensures the restoration of the political letter and both secrets are preserved.

Here the text is symmetrically elusive concerning both sexuality and politics. Watson, as is so often the case where these areas are concerned, begins the story by apologizing for his own reticence and vagueness. In the political instance what becomes clear as a result of the uncertainty of the text is the contradictory nature of the requirements of verisimilitude in fiction. The potentate's identity and the nature of his indiscretion cannot be named without involving on the part of the reader either disbelief (the introduction of a patently fictional country would be dangerous to the project of verisimilitude) or belief (dangerous to the text's status as fiction, entertainment; also quite possibly politically dangerous). The scientific project of the texts require that they deal in 'facts', but their nature as fiction forbids the introduction of actual facts.

The classic realist text installs itself in the space between fact and illusion through the presentation of a simulated reality which is plausible but *not real*. In this lies its power as myth. It is because fiction does not normally deal with 'politics' directly, except in the form of history or satire, that it is ostensibly innocent and therefore ideologically effective. But in its evasion of the real also lies its weakness as 'realism'. Through their transgression of their own values of explicitness and verisimilitude, the Sherlock Holmes stories contain within themselves an implicit critique of their limited nature as characteristic examples of classic realism. They thus offer the reader, through the process of reading as work, a form of knowledge, not about 'life' or 'the world', but about the nature of fiction itself.

Thus, in adopting the form of classic realism, the only appropriate literary mode, positivism is compelled to display its own limitations.

Offered as science, it reveals itself to such a reading as ideology at the very moment that classic realism, offered as verisimilitude, reveals itself as fiction. In claiming to make explicit and *understandable* what appears mysterious, these texts offer evidence of the tendency of positivism to push to the margins of experience whatever it cannot explain or understand. In the Sherlock Holmes stories classic realism ironically tells a truth, though not the truth about the world which is the project of classic realism. The truth the stories tell is the truth about ideology, the truth which ideology represses, its own existence as ideology itself.

'THE SCHOLAR-GIPSY'

If the central project of the Sherlock Holmes stories is to *dispel* mystery in the name of science, the project of the Romantic ode is the quite antithetical one of *revealing* the mystery at the heart of things, the intense and visionary core of subjective experience which makes possible escape from the drab routine of everyday externality. Wordsworth's 'Intimations of Immortality', Coleridge's 'Kubla Khan', Shelley's 'Ode to the West Wind', Keats's 'Ode to a Nightingale' and 'Ode on a Grecian Urn' all to varying degrees attempt to isolate the moment of vision which is itself the source of poetry, and to meditate on the meaning and value of the vision-as-poem. In 'Kubla Khan', the 'Nightingale' and the 'Grecian Urn' the source of the vision – and its symbol in the poem – is itself a form of art (song, the urn), and the poet, in re-producing the visionary experience, produces poetry.

Arnold's 'Scholar-Gipsy' is in many senses the culmination of this tradition. The poem is an appeal to a shepherd (reader?) to leave, when night falls, the everyday world of work, and join the poet in his quest for the elusive scholar who, 'tired of knocking at preferment's door', has rejected the 'real conditions' of Victorian England, evoked in images of illness:

> . . . this strange disease of modern life,
>   With its sick hurry, its divided aims,
>   Its heads o'ertaxed, its palsied hearts . . .

'The Scholar-Gipsy' alludes most directly to the 'Ode to a Nightingale':

the stanza form is similar; lines and images echo Keats ('our feverish contact'; 'But thou possessest an immortal lot'); and above all the descriptions of natural plenitude evoke the celebrated fifth stanza of Keats's poem. But 'The Scholar-Gipsy' shares the common Romantic rejection of the world created by industrial capitalism, the drab, mechanical and competitive life of the dim city, deadly to its inhabitants both morally and physically.

Poetry is seen by contrast as the source of 'intimations of immortality'. The scholar-gipsy is himself a poet-figure, seeking the immortal poetic vision, 'Rapt, twirling in thy hand a withered spray, / And waiting for the spark from heaven to fall'. He seeks from the gipsies the secret of their art, a power to bind discursively 'the workings of men's brains'.

The Romantic project necessitates not realist prose, of course, but poetry, in which connotative and symbolic meanings conventionally prevail over denotation and in which, therefore, the mysterious and the magical are appropriately suggested. In the Romantic ode poetry enshrines the record of its own birth. The account of the vision is the poem itself and therefore it is the poem which constitutes the proof of the validity of the vision, the truth of the intimations of immortality which the text records. The poem then generates in the reader a participation in these intimations, and this is the source of its power to transcend and transform the world, to redeem it from death. In Shelley's version the West Wind symbolizes both the poetic vision which is to bring life to the poet and the 'incantation' of the poem itself which will 'quicken a new birth' in the dying world. The poem is thus a perfect circle, autonomous and self-contained, emblem and evidence of its own values, immortalizing the ephemeral vision and so offering the gift of life to its readers.

'The Scholar-Gipsy' takes this project to an extreme. The scholar-gipsy, the poem's central symbol for the poet, is himself immortalized in a 'tale', Glanvil's book, which lies beside the poet-speaker in his pastoral retreat. The scholar-gipsy, literally long-dead, lives on Glanvil's page, and re-lives in Arnold's poem, immortal emblem of the values he represents.

At this point, however, an uneasiness appears in the poem's logic (Wilkenfeld 1969: 126). That characters in books cannot die is unexceptionable, but the Romantic project requires a stronger claim, that the scholar-gipsy as poet lives not only in the pages of another writer but in his own right, for only in this way does he constitute an emblem of the power of poetry to give life to the world. And here the poem becomes more uncertain as it becomes more argumentative, less 'poetic'. Stanzas 14–17 first assert that Glanvil's story is two hundred years old, that the scholar-gipsy is dead: 'And thou from earth art gone/Long since, and in some quiet churchyard laid'. But then follows an immediate reversal: 'No, no, thou hast not felt the lapse of hours'. The tenses in the following stanza shift uneasily in describing this figure who is dead and not dead: 'Thou hast not lived, why should'st thou perish so?/Thou had'st one aim . . .' 'Hast', 'had'st': the scholar-gipsy belongs only uncertainly to the present. At last it appears that his claim to live depends not merely on Glanvil's book but on his own withdrawal from the world: 'For early did'st thou leave the world, with powers/Fresh, undiverted to the world without. . . .' His pursuit of the poetic vision depends on evasion of the world of distraction and doubt. That he has not yet learned to rule the workings of men's brains, become an unacknowledged legislator of the world, as Shelley puts it, this same distraction and doubt which is the disease of society conclusively demonstrates. But in these circumstances the scholar-gipsy, waiting for the 'spark from heaven', cannot constitute an emblem of the power of poetry to immortalize in art the moment of poetic vision and so to transform the world.

The dissatisfaction of the text with the logic of its own argument in this central section is everywhere apparent. The main symbol of the poem, the scholar-gipsy himself, is insubstantial, elusive and finally absent. The quest so eagerly begun is unfulfilled: the scholar-gipsy is only fleetingly glimpsed by others, not seen at all by the speaker. The poet ends by urging him, 'fly our paths, our feverish contact fly'. Finally the scholar-gipsy indeed disappears from the poem. The concluding image substitutes the heroic figure of the Tyrian trader, untainted by the uncertainties revealed earlier in the poem, but drawn from the remote past, neither a poet nor immortal, and thus largely irrelevant to the initial project of the text.

The imagery of the poem seeks uneasily for modes of signification which will do justice to the nature of the poetic vision. The poem begins in the pastoral mode, then abandons this and moves through a series of images of natural plenitude which are the setting for the elusive scholar-gipsy, and which have the paradoxical effect of emphasizing by their richness his virtual absence from the text. Finally the image of the Tyrian trader produces an illusion of closure, an *ad hoc* optimism only tenuously related to the total organization of the poem. Because it confronts them with integrity, the text therefore contradicts its own claims on behalf of poetry. Unable to show the scholar-gipsy or his immortal vision, it is not able to provide the evidence it seeks of the power of poetry to give life to the world.

'The Scholar-Gipsy' is not an isolated case: affirmation is repeatedly qualified or undermined in Romantic verse. In Wordsworth's 'Ode: Intimations of Immortality' a related contradiction makes doubt the source of knowledge. Here the vision, origin of the power truly to 'see', is not, when we finally reach it, an experience of radiant light, as the imagery of the poem has led us to expect. On the contrary, it is a radical uncertainty, evoked primarily in negatives, a series of encounters with the unknown and unidentifiable which becomes the source of deathless truths:

> Not for these I raise
> The song of thanks and praise;
> But for those obstinate questionings
> Of sense and outward things,
> Fallings from us, vanishings;
> Blank misgivings of a Creature
> Moving about in worlds not realised,
> High instincts, before which our mortal Nature
> Did tremble like a guilty Thing surprised:
> But for those first affections,
> Those shadowy recollections,
> Which, be they what they may,
> Are yet the fountain light of all our day,
> Are yet a master light of all our seeing;
> Uphold us, cherish, and have power to make
> Our noisy years seem moments in the being
> Of the eternal Silence: truths that wake,
> To perish never.

In Keats's 'Ode to a Nightingale' the escape from mortality is to a world of mutability. The nightingale's 'happy' song becomes a 'requiem' and finally a 'plaintive anthem', and the transcendent vision succeeds only in recalling the world of loss which was its antithesis. Here the text is explicit. The nightingale's song evokes 'fairy lands forlorn'.

> Forlorn. The very word is like a bell
> To toll me back from thee to my sole self.

One of the main thrusts of Romanticism is the rejection of an alien world of industrial capitalism, recurrently signified in images of death, disease and decay. Poetry claims to create a living world, fostered by nature but springing essentially from the subjectivity of the poet, from what Coleridge calls the Imagination, a mode of perception which endows the phenomenal world with a vitality and an intensity issuing ultimately from the soul itself: 'Oh Lady! we receive but what we give,/ And in our life alone does Nature live' ('Dejection: an Ode'). The Romantic vision, though it needs the phenomenal world for its realization, transcends and transforms the material and the mortal.

The Romantic rejection of the 'real conditions' is based on a belief in the autonomy of the subject. The 'man possessed of more than usual organic sensibility' greets in solitude the experiences he himself generates. But the escape, the transcendence, is rapidly seen to double back on itself: the higher knowledge proves to be a dream or a reversion to the very reality whose antithesis it was to represent. In the absence of an adequate theory of the subject as the individual in society, a meeting-place of the network of linguistic relationships which articulate experience, the Romantics were unable to account for this doubling back, experiencing it only as loss or betrayal of the vision. Much of the poetry of the nineteenth and early twentieth centuries constitutes a record of increasing despair as the contradictions in the Romantic rejection of the world became increasingly manifest. Unable to theorize the inadequacy of its concept of subjectivity (and committed, indeed, to experience as against theory), the poetry can ultimately only present the subject as trapped between intolerable alternatives, the mortality of the material world and what Yeats calls the 'cold snows of a dream'. Romanticism in poetry, like the positivism of classic realism, provides, precisely through the determination and integrity with which it pursues its project, evidence of the uncertainty of its own undertaking. The Romantic ode, celebration of the presence of subjectivity, moves towards a formal centre which is to be the emblem of its own theme, the embodiment of the vision which is its source. What it finds there is a central absence, a radical inconsistency which leads either to elegy or to interrogation in the place of the awaited triumph at the moment of closure: 'Fled is that music. . . . Do I wake or sleep?'

The Lacanian subject is constructed on the basis of a splitting which is irreversible. The jubilation of the mirror-phase is also an alienation, the moment of division between the I which perceives and the perceived (imaged) I. Much of Romantic poetry records a quest for the lost wholeness and transcendence of the imaginary, an attempt to find in nature a mirror which will reflect an image of the subject at one with itself and its context, a unity that precedes differences. But subjectivity is predicated on difference and the imaginary unity is for ever elusive. The scholar-gipsy, mirror-image of the poet, is whole, untainted, transcendent, immortal, long-lost, dead, never to be found. His substitute in the economy of the poem is the Tyrian trader, heroic parallel and contrast to the traders of Victorian England. In refusing the real conditions created by the industrial revolution, 'The Scholar-Gipsy' paradoxically takes as its project an affirmation of the transcendent subject of liberal humanism which is the ideological ally of industrial capitalism. The formal absence at the centre of the poem offers the reader a knowledge of the lack which is the condition of precisely that subjectivity.

7

DECONSTRUCTION AND THE DIFFERANCE IT MAKES

SAUSSURE REVISITED

A year after *A Theory of Literary Production* and three years before *S/Z*, Jacques Derrida reread Saussure in the context of a book about writing. In 1967 *Of Grammatology* analysed the implications of the tendency of Western culture to privilege speech over the written text. This apparently innocent issue opened the way for a challenge to Western metaphysics in its entirety.

Metaphysics is the study of foundations, the grounds on which specific knowledges are based. The ground, explanation and ultimate recourse of the religions of the Book, for example, is God; science, by contrast, takes the laws of nature as given and as the support and guarantee of all the truths it uncovers; Western philosophy, meanwhile, appeals to reason as the authority which is not itself open to question. Each system is constructed on the basis of these presupposed foundations. Derrida's conclusion in *Of Grammatology*, however, was that no such foundations existed, and his reading of Saussure's *Course in General Linguistics* played a major part in the argument.

The Course represented a radical challenge to meptaphysics, Derrida maintained, in its introduction of the signifier, which took the place of the conventional sign as the sign of an idea or thing, believed to exist as a unit outside language. Even though his account of the signifier dislodged the assumption that language named given entities, however, Saussure did not adequately repudiate the unexamined *phonocentrism* of his culture, the conviction that writing was no more than an imitation of speech. On the contrary, Derrida pointed out, he took a remarkably strong phonocentric line: writing was not merely a copy of speech; it was also, Saussure declared, tyrannical, unnatural, perverse, pathological, sinful. The vocabulary of *The Course* seems to denounce writing in excess of any crime it could possibly be held to commit. But in this respect *The Course* was not, *Grammatology* was able to show, all that exceptional. Western philosophy has always tended to see writing as no more than the transcription of speech, in a binary opposition which values speech as the thing itself, genuine, authentic, while writing is at best derivative, and at worst a betrayal of the immediacy of speech.

Why is writing condemned so vehemently? Because, Derrida argues, it constitutes a threat to the metaphysics phonocentrism supports. Writing goes on signifying in the absence not only of the referent, the topic it concerns, but of the signatory, the writer. Phonocentrism appeals to the mind of the speaker, and the world of things the speaker shares with his or her interlocutors, as the twin guarantees of meaning, where meaning is understood to be the experiential truth 'expressed' in an account of the world. But writing self-evidently continues to mean (if not to mean exactly the same) across time and space. The writer might be dead; the world described might be an unknown continent or a remote historical period present to the writer but not to us; the description does not in consequence become meaning-less, however.

Writing, therefore, which demonstrates that signification does not depend on the presence of its topic, or the writer's ideas of the topic, writing as 'the name of these two absences' (Derrida 1997a: 41), challenges Western *logocentrism*, the attribution of primacy to ideas. Logocentrism asssumes that ideas come first; speech is an 'expression', an uttered (outered) copy, of our ideas of things; and writing is a copy of a copy. But if we reject the phonocentric illusion that writing is inferior, fallen from the grace of speech, which is already fallen from the first perfection of the idea, then the presence of ideas themselves as pristine intelligibility, the transcendental products of consciousness, necessarily comes into question. Brought to confront the more radical aspects of Saussure's *Course*, logocentrism loses all credibility, since ideas appear as effects of the signifier, not its cause.

But if ideas are effects, and not origins, those foundational, transcendental ideas, God, nature and reason, lose their capacity to guarantee meaning and truth. We long, but in vain, for a free-standing, self-guaranteeing signified, an Idea, that would hold all other meanings in place, but no such transcendental signified exists. Thought is not finally anchored in anything outside the differences, without positive terms, which constitute the language that enables us to think in the first place.

DECONSTRUCTION

The logic of Derrida's position depends, however, not on critique, the traditional practice of Western philosophy, which seeks the flaw in the argument as a basis for repudiating the analysis. Instead of triumphantly casting *The Course* aside, Derrida adopts the practice of demonstrating by a very close reading of the text itself that the oppositions which structure its argument do not hold. In Saussure's case, the binary opposition between innocent speech and corrupt writing does not stay in place. The excess evident in Saussure's vocabulary, the perverse and unnatural 'tyranny' he attributes to writing, defines a particularly powerful threat because, it turns out, he sees writing as tyrannizing *over* speech. Speech, pure and selfsame, is subject to *invasion* by writing, its differentiating other. Spelling, the written form, Saussure reveals with disgust, influences pronunciation, the spoken form. People *speak differently* in consequence of writing: the written makes itself felt in speech.

Deconstruction identifies the invasion of the other into the selfsame. And it maintains that this invasion is always inevitable in the light of Saussure's own account of meaning as the effect of difference. Saussure is thus not rejected. If his own work is brought into play to undo the logic of his existing argument, the radical elements of that argument go on to become components of an alternative position which is more radical still. Opposed meanings, Derrida affirms, are never pure, pristine or autonomous. The signifier signifies, but it does so not by reference to some imagined selfsame signified, a freestanding idea, the independent product of consciousness, but instead on the sole basis of difference. In *The Course* itself, for example, speech-as-privileged, speech as what is valued in a phonocentric world, is *what is not written*. But this meaning of speech, its intelligibility, depends, therefore, on the trace of the excluded term, writing. We owe meaning, here as elsewhere, to the trace of the other in the selfsame.

DIFFERANCE

We owe it, in other words, to the trace *and no more*. The chapter of *Grammatology* on Saussure also invokes the term *differance*, spelt with an *a*, but this Derridean coinage is explained in more detail in the essay, 'Differance', first delivered as a lecture in 1968, shortly after the publication of *Grammatology*.

One of the translators of this essay left the word in 'French' (though it did not exist in French before Derrida devised it) and many of Derrida's English-speaking admirers have followed suit, but in the process they lose the Saussurean and deconstructive joke inscribed in Derrida's invention of the term. The point, Derrida patiently explains, is that 'differance' sounds no different from 'difference', and to use the term in a lecture, to *speak* it, he will have to invoke the spelling if he wants to be understood. He will have to say 'with an *a*' or 'with an *e*' (1973: 132–3). Meaning depends on difference; at the same time, written spelling invades speech.

Not a word in any existing language, differance is not a concept either. Coinage discourages the notion that signifiers name pre-existing ideas. What, then, is differance, if the term is not in consequence meaning-less? The French verb *différer* means both to differ, as in English, and to defer, literally to put off, to postpone, to subject completion or accomplishment to a detour. Meaning depends on difference. Could it also be said to involve deferral?

If we go back to the traditional account of meaning, by which the sign stands in for an idea or a thing, we see that the sign takes the place of this idea or thing, re-presents it, makes it present to imagination in its absence. The sign, in the classical account, suspends the presence of the idea or thing, replaces it, and in the process pushes it away. The sign represents a detour which defers presence.

If, on the other hand, in accordance with *The Course*, language does not name pre-existing entities, if in language there are only differences, if ideas (or things) do not have primacy, then meaning, or the signified, is not in itself a presence. But, brought into conceptual being by the signifier, the meaning is not an absence either. Instead, it can be understood as a deferred presence, a presence relegated, pushed away and replaced by the signifier.

Differance, then, neither active nor passive, but with an *a* like 'resonance' or 'perseverance', gives rise to meaning. How? Neither an action nor a state of being, differance represents a process, movement. This movement, deferring, relegating, supplanting, the 'play' that produces the differences, while itself not a concept, not 'full' of presence, is not empty either. Differance is meaning's only, 'nonfull, nonsimple "origin"' (Derrida 1973: 141).

UNDECIDABILITY

'*The trace is in fact the absolute origin of sense in general. Which amounts to saying once again that there is no absolute origin of sense in general. The trace is the differance* which opens appearance [*l'apparaître*] and signification' (Derrida 1997a: 65). If the trace of the other in the selfsame is the condition of the possibility of meaning, it follows that meaning is never pure, never absolute. Inevitably invaded by what it sets out to exclude, any proposition is shadowed by its differentiating other.

This does not imply a confusion of meaning, still less that any meaning is as pertinent as any other, the free-for-all of the 'anything goes' that Derrida's opponents claim to find in his work. On the contrary. But it does suggest that the sharply posed alternatives of absolute certainty will not hold, that meaning and truth are *undecidable* as between identifiable and opposed poles.

How does this relate to the political analyses of Roland Barthes, Pierre Macherey and Louis Althusser? In the first place, it confirms the relativity of what we seem to know, and further undermines the knowing subject of the liberal humanist tradition, in possession of the truth derived from an accurate understanding of the objects of knowledge. While rejecting the 'metaphysical' aspects of psychoanalysis, the unconscious as a presence, repository of demons capable of being brought to light in analysis, Derrida identifies the unconscious as a 'radical alterity' that takes away, detracts from every process of representation (1973: 151–2), destabilizing what we think we know for sure.

As their contemporary, the Derrida of the 1960s took a differential position, especially from the Marxism of Macherey and Althusser. In his own philosophy, no direct party affiliation was evident. But much of his later work has been concerned with the political implications of deconstruction. In *Specters of Marx*, written after the fall of the Berlin Wall had apparently discredited Marxism, he challenged the triumphalist affirmation of universal capitalism, which remains, he claims, haunted by the ghost of its rejected Marxist antagonist (1994).

Insisting on the difference within identity, deconstruction also calls into question identity politics, all forms of nationalism, and all totalitarianisms.

> Sometimes the struggles under the banner of cultural identity, national identity, linguistic identity, are noble fights. But at the same time the people who fight for their identity must pay attention to the fact that identity is not the self-identity of a thing ... but implies a difference within identity. That is, the identity of a culture is a way of being different from itself; a culture is different from itself; language is different from itself; the person is different from itself.
>
> (Caputo 1997: 13)

Is deconstruction, then, a justification of inertia? On the contrary, Derrida answers: 'it is the only way for me to take responsibility and to make decisions' (14). The twentieth century offers many examples of the importance of that stance.

'EASTER 1916'

On Monday 24 April 1916 a group of men, led by Patrick Pearse of the Volunteers, a secret army within the Irish Republican Brotherhood, took possession of the General Post Office in Dublin and proclaimed the Irish Republic. The Volunteers, in conjunction with the Citizen Army, under the militant trade unionist, James Connolly, also seized other strategic buildings in Dublin, where they held out against British troops until the following Sunday.

The original Rising had been planned, in a sort of performative pun, for Easter Sunday, but was postponed when the efforts of Sir Roger Casement to land supporting weapons from Germany fell through. The Rising took place in the middle of the First World War. British reprisals against what was perceived as treason were swift and ruthless. In the first two weeks of May 1916 fifteen leaders of the rebellion were summarily shot.

If the Rising took the British by surprise, most of Ireland was even more astonished by the events in Dublin. The partition of the island was the main issue at this time between Unionists, most of them Protestants, and the Catholic majority, committed to Home Rule, a form of devolution which would confer on an Irish parliament responsibility for internal affairs. Home Rule had finally been enacted by the British Parliament in 1914, but its implementation was put off in the national crisis created by the War. Over a quarter of a million of the Irish served with British forces. In 1916 the Irish Republican Brotherhood had about two thousand members, and not all of these were in favour of the Rising, which was thus planned and executed by 'a minority of a minority' (Foster 1988: 475).[1]

In purely military terms, the Rising achieved virtually nothing. And yet arguably it changed the course of history. How should we interpret it? As the founding moment of Irish independence? As the mystical rebirth of Irish nationalism through blood sacrifice? As the inaugural moment of a cult of death that would be invoked to legitimate a century of IRA violence against Britain? Was it a heroic stand against oppression, or a foolhardy and unnecessary waste of energy and idealism?

In September the same year W. B. Yeats completed his poem, 'Easter 1916', which concludes with an implicit appeal, in the names of the protagonists of the Rising, to an Irish future that is, like the rebels themselves, transformed irrevocably:

> MacDonagh and MacBride
> And Connolly and Pearse
> Now and in time to be,
> Wherever green is worn,
> Are changed, changed utterly:
> A terrible beauty is born.

But the final oxymoron that recurs as a kind of refrain throughout the poem, bringing beauty into conjunction with terror, calls into question any easy characterization of the Rising's consequences. What judgement is made here? What is the 'terrible beauty' that has been given such painful birth?

The poem puzzles it out, as if seeking to assign the event to one side or the other of a binary line. Were the rebels heroes? – Constance Markiewicz, the 'shrill' polemicist; Pearse, the schoolmaster and poet; Thomas MacDonagh, whose life seemed full of promise; and John MacBride, 'A drunken, vainglorious lout'. Or were they instead fanatics, their hearts reduced to stone by a fixed, obsessional, deadly allegiance, indifferent to the living, changing stream of life?

And if they were thus bound to death by their own convictions, who was to blame? Their own blindness, or an oppressor that refused to be appeased? 'Too long a sacrifice / Can make a stone of the heart. / O when may it suffice?' Was the sacrifice worth making, or did the rebels simply misjudge the moment, the situation, British policy? 'Was it needless death after all? / For England may keep faith / For all that is done and said.' Were they fooled in this, moreover, by their own fervent Irish patriotism? 'And what if excess of love / Bewildered them till they died?'

How, in turn, should we as readers understand the force of that, 'What if . . . ?'? Does the phrase register, as in surprise, the reluctant recognition of an appalling possibility: 'what if they were merely bewildered?'? Or does it, conversely, dismiss the question as irrelevant in the light of their heroism: 'what (does it matter) if they were bewildered?'? In a poem that does its best to set heroism against fanaticism, change against fixity, and life against death, signifying practice itself equivocates, refuses the univocity of a single meaning or a single judgement.

What, then, should we see as the character of the 'terrible beauty' born from their executions? Is it the example to future generations of their Christ-like sacrifice, or the resurrection of 'romantic Ireland', which Yeats himself had previously proclaimed dead and gone in his poem 'September 1913'? The phrase treats the death of the rebels as a source of life, a birth, and replaces the 'Minute by minute' change that characterizes the everyday with an apocalyptic transformation that fixes or monumentalizes their names, both in the poem and beyond it.

The text, called 'Easter 1916', is strangely silent about the details of the Rising. The seizure of the Post Office, the Proclamation of the Republic, and the recapture of the buildings are not mentioned. Perhaps they can be taken for granted? In any case, all the textual attention is focused on the ideals of the rebels and their deaths: 'enough / To know they dreamed and are dead'. The occurrence the poem memorializes is this dream and its consequences, the reprisals. The punishment ensures that the oppositions the poem has struggled to set up, between fanaticism and heroism, fixity and flux, death and life, do not hold. By arresting the gradual changes of ordinary life, imposing fixity, bringing life out of death, the executions *make* heroes, whose names, murmured, recited, written out in a verse, defer, relegate and supplant their qualities as individuals. On this analysis, heroism is not a characteristic possessed by a person, but a condition, a name, conferred by events, and by the textuality of a poem.

Running through 'Easter 1916' is a self-referential opposition between comic narrative and epic poetry. On the one hand, before the Rising the rebels themselves, with their 'vivid faces', so incongruous in the grey streets of Dublin, had appeared no more than material for 'a mocking tale or a gibe' to be told at the club, since the demise of romantic Ireland had reduced her, in a reference to the classic garment of the Fool, to no more than a place 'where motley is worn'. On the other hand, even MacBride, transformed in spite of himself, now takes his place in another genre: 'I number him in the song; / He, too, has resigned his part / In the casual comedy'. Conventionally, epic does not probe the nicely calculated less or more of ethical judgement, but names heroic figures and lists their grand exploits. Is 'Easter 1916' Ireland's *Iliad*?

> I write it out in a verse –
> MacDonagh and MacBride
> And Connolly and Pearse
> Now and in time to be,
> Wherever green is worn,
> Are changed, changed utterly.

'Now and in time to be' is the tense of epic, which conventionally records inaugural moments, and identifies its protagonists as exemplary figures for the future, models for aspiration.

Epic, indeed, would dissolve the poem's uncertainties in a final affirmation, were it not for the fact that the last line reiterates the oxymoronic 'terrible beauty', and thus reintroduces the undecidability that characterizes so much of the text. And besides, nothing could be less epic in manner than the spare, almost conversational trimeter of poem itself. It is this austerity that throws into relief the 'terrible beauty', which itself performs at the level of the signifier the transformation it also records.

The recurring phrase evokes not epic so much as the Aristotelean pity and fear of tragedy, and this, in its low-key, modernist form, is surely the genre of 'Easter 1916'. Tragedy, which classically attributes a kind of wisdom to the Fool, and ennobles the erring, is the genre of undecidability above all. Are Oedipus and Antigone, Lear and Hedda Gabler driven by heroism or folly? Are their deaths exemplary, or a cruel waste of misdirected energy? Tragedy raises the questions, but without minimizing their significance, withholds final answers, refusing to resolve uncertainty. Tragedy defers, without suspending it, ethical and political judgement.

At the same time, modern Irish drama, from J. M. Synge's *The Playboy of the Western World* through Sean O'Casey and Samuel Beckett to Martin McDonagh, characteristically deconstructs the opposition between tragedy and comedy, intensifying the undecidability in the process. Whichever we perceive the plays to be, the other genre devastatingly invades the selfsame, not only making a mockery of conventional classification, but leaving the meaning of the play to an exceptional degree unresolved. Intimately related to this tradition, 'Easter 1916' is also, in its own way, generically and thematically unsettling.

THE VERDICT OF HISTORY

Michael Collins also compared the Easter Rising to a Greek tragedy (Foster 1988: 483). The subsequent historiography of the Rising has been on the whole no more decisive in its verdict than Yeats's poem. The consensus, if there is one, has been that the Rising led directly to the replacement of the Home Rule project by republicanism. In the election of 1918 Sinn Féin won 73 seats, as against the Irish Parliamentary Party's six. National independence was now the widely shared project of Catholic Ireland.

But if the Rising brought this about, it did so to some degree inadvertently. It was not self-evident what the target had been: the British state, which was already committed to Home Rule, the half-heartedness of the Irish Parliamentary Party itself, or the threat of partition to appease the Unionists. But the remorselessness of the reprisals focused hostility on Britain, and this, in conjunction with a mounting fear of compulsory military service in the British war against Germany, in due course cemented informed Irish opinion in favour of independence.

THE LAW OF THE DECISION

Paradoxically, the decision to act is always incommensurable with the grounds that justify it. We take a position, Derrida argues, not because thought leads to certainty, or because what we know leads inevitably to a single conclusion. If the conclusion were inevitable, the outcome would not be a 'decision'. What, then, are the political implications of undecidability?

Deconstruction might, of course, look like a reason for refusing to take a position, for remaining neutral. But neutrality is not in practice neutral at all, since it leaves things as they were, or as they would have been anyway. Neutrality makes decisions, but always for the status quo.

A decision is prompted by circumstances. At a specific moment it becomes imperative either to act or not to act, to take a position or not to take a position, when not to take a position is also to decide. In that sense, the decision is not in practice the outcome of the thought which has led up to it, but is always a matter of urgency:

> Centuries of preparatory reflection and theoretical deliberation – the very infinity of a knowledge – would change nothing in this urgency. It is absolutely cutting, conclusive, decisive, heartrending; it must interrupt the time of science and conscience, to which the instant of decision will always remain heterogeneous.
>
> (Derrida 1997b: 79)

Does it follow that decisions are properly, appropriately or inevitably irresponsible? On the contrary. But they necessarily involve a risk. To take responsibility is always to take a risk, precisely because a stance that is no more than the outcome of a prior knowledge cannot be seen as our own responsibility. We must at all costs avoid, Derrida announces dismissively, the security of 'good conscience'.

Is this view explicable in terms of an adopted aristocratic Romanticism, comparable to the stance some would attribute to Yeats? Not at all. Instead, it has its own logic:

> To protect the decision or the responsibility by knowledge, by some theoretical assurance, or by the certainty of being right, of being on the side of science, of consciousness or of reason, is to transform this experience into the deployment of a program, into a technical application of a rule or a norm, or into the subsumption of a determined 'case'.

> (Derrida 1993: 19)

In other words, to safeguard the decision by a prior certainty is, paradoxically, to evade responsibility, to hand over responsibility to a rule, an outside force, an organization, a dogma. Responsibility is always – and by definition – personal.

Is it therefore arbitrary? Not in the least. Only binary thinking would pose the alternatives in this form. Derrida's analysis deconstructs the opposition between certainty and arbitrariness. We do the best we can in the light of what it is possible to know. In the absence of a metaphysics which would relieve us of the obligation to decide and remove personal responsibility, certainty is not an option. Decisions are made in the light of undecidability; they necessarily entail risk.

Perhaps prompted in the first instance by undecidability, the Easter Rising remains itself undecidable. It was conceivably 'needless', quite possibly folly. But like the protagonists of tragedy, the rebels took a risk, and in the process they took responsibility for a moment of history. Yeats's poem might be read as proposing that, in the end, it is not for those who stood by, either then or now, to close off the implications of that moment by subsuming it under the binary options of a legalistic moral and political verdict.

8

TOWARDS A PRODUCTIVE CRITICAL PRACTICE

READERS AS CONSUMERS

The critical quest for expressive realism acts as the ally of classic realism in constructing the reader as consumer. On the other hand 'the goal of literary work (of literature as work) is to make the reader no longer a consumer, but a producer of the text' (Barthes 1975: 4). Barthes owes to Brecht the distinction he makes here between the passive consumer of the readable (*lisible*) classic realist text and the active producer of meaning who accepts the challenge of the writable (*scriptible*) text. Brecht distinguishes between the audience of traditional 'dramatic theatre', supine, motionless, apparently in a trance, and the alert, thoughtful spectators of his own 'epic theatre', actively engaged in the work of criticizing the play of contradictions on the stage (Brecht 1964: 187). Despite the recognition Brecht has received, and despite his undoubted influence on the forms of European theatre, the spectator or reader as consumer remains the norm in our society. Dramatic theatre (now mediated by television) and the classic realist novel are still the dominant popular modes. The cinema, too, is still dominated by narrative illusionism in spite of the efforts of an active avant-garde.

For this reason it is perhaps worth developing the analogy between readers (or spectators) and consumers. Indeed, analogy is too weak a term: books are literally commodities, of course, but the ideology of literary criticism places the reader more decisively in the position of consumer – consumer of a 'spiritual' value which constitutes a displacement of the idea of the value of a commodity. No doubt readers have always preferred some books to others, but it was the Romantic movement, contemporary with the rise of industrial capitalism, which initiated the process of endowing certain texts with a worth that had little to do with mere enjoyment but depended instead on a magical and timeless value inherent only in great art.

The distribution system in the form in which it has developed in capitalism has the effect of suppressing the process of production. Goods are displayed in shop windows, catalogues or magazines, often in settings which simulate the conditions (or an idealized version of the conditions) in which they will be used. Commodities are seen in their finished form among other commodities and not in the context of the factories in which they were made. Industrial areas of towns are located away from shopping areas. Even those advertisements which draw attention to the high technology or skill involved in the production process tend to do so by showing pictures of scientists in white coats, or craftsmen with chisels. They do not show workers and conveyor belts on the shop floor. The labour involved in production is suppressed, and the process itself is either mystified or ignored.

A precisely similar suppression occurs in conventional literary criticism. The literary text is seen not as a construct, the result of a process, but as the natural reflection of the world it delineates or the spontaneous expression of its author's subjectivity. Of course, literary biographies concede that authors work to produce texts, just as we know that commodities are made in factories. Nevertheless, the emphasis of criticism is not on the text as constructed artifact but on its truth or its expressiveness. The process of production is called creation, a mystical and mysterious occurrence conceived rather as a state of mind than as work. As a result, conventional criticism gazes in awe at the finished product, whose value resides above all in its status as embodiment of the author's genius.

The effect is an illusion of complicity between the author and the reader. The text is an invisible thread leading from the author's subjectivity to the reader's. The author's name on the cover, known, established, famous, is the guarantee of access to his or her imagination, just as the brand name of the product guarantees the quality of the commodity. But the brand name on the product is the name of the employer or the company, not of the workers whose labour produced it. In a similar way, the author's name evokes given essences, qualities of insight and understanding, and not the labour of producing out of the available signifying systems of language and literature an intelligible fiction. The neglect of this – not of the private experience of the individual author as worker, but of the mode of production itself, the materials and their arrangement in the work – leads to a literary criticism which in the last analysis is not itself productive. Expressive-realist criticism is finally parasitic on literature, unable to distance itself from literature to the point where it has an independent process of production to perform. Ultimately expressive-realist criticism can only reproduce the (itself ideologically produced) 'experience' of reading the text, and then comment, 'Yes, that's how it is; I feel it', or 'that is not it at all'.

This last purely intuitive distinction then becomes the basis of a set of value judgements which constitute the central object of criticism. Review pages and departments of literature come to function like consumers' associations whose main purpose is to write reports advising readers on the best (spiritual) buys, with additional details concerning, for instance, the distinctions between short-term topical worth and longer-term intellectual investment. Its value, usually seen as universal and eternal, inheres in the text itself, and the reading process mysteriously transmits this essence to the reader. Criticism, presented as non-theoretical, neutral and objective, is seen as facilitating this transmission process, impartially advising and assisting the reader to derive the maximum benefit from the (freely chosen) commodity.

Althusser proposes that the task of ideology is to conceal its own role in reproducing the conditions of the capitalist mode of production, and it is here that we reach a way of accounting for the impoverished role of conventional literary criticism. If ideology is a set of omissions, gaps, and partial truths, then ideological criticism may be understood as a source of partial analysis of literary texts, concealing and obscuring more than it reveals. In suppressing the process and conditions of production of literary texts, criticism also suppresses their role in helping to create a world of autonomous subjects who 'work by themselves' in subjection to the existing social formation.

The strategies of the classic realist text divert the reader from what is contradictory within it to the renewed recognition (misrecognition) of what he or she already 'knows', knows because the myths and signifying systems of the classic realist text re-present experience in the ways in which it is conventionally articulated in our society. A post-Saussurean criticism, on the other hand, distancing itself from the imaginary coherence of the text, analysing the language which is its material and the process of production which makes it a text, recognizes in the text not 'knowledge', but ideology itself in all its inconsistency and partiality. To avoid this analysis, ideology needs an inert and unproductive criticism as the text's accomplice in ensuring the role of the reader as consumer. Ignoring the process of production of the text, dazzled by its brand name, and preoccupied by the assessment of its value, the reader is effectively diverted from the work of producing the play of contradictions which in practice constitutes the literary text.

Brecht's solution was to write a new kind of text, foregrounding contradiction rather than effacing it, and distancing the audience from both text and ideology. In what I have called the interrogative text there is no simple hierarchy of voices such that the reader is offered privileged access to the work's 'truth'. Instead the reader constructs meaning out of the contradictory voices which the text provides. Barthes speaks of the multiplicity of voices of indeterminate origin in the writable text, the polyphony which deprives the implied author of authority so that the truth of any one of the voices is not guaranteed by a knowledge of its origin or source (Barthes 1975: 41–2).

The problem here is that it seems that none the less any text can be rendered fit for consumption. Brecht's plays have become classics of the bourgeois theatre. Polyphony does not guarantee that readers will recognize the plurality of voices: a convention of reading in quest of statements, messages, the author's knowledge, can lead readers to select and privilege one of the voices of the text, one of its narratives. And if this fails, a critical industry is available to explain the (single) meaning of texts like *Gulliver's Travels* or *The Winter's Tale*.

The solution, then, must be not only a new mode of writing but also a new critical practice, which insists on finding the plurality, however 'parsimonious', of the text and refuses the pseudo-dominance constructed as the 'obvious' position of its intelligibility by the forms of classic realism. As readers and critics, we can choose actively to seek out the process of production of the text: the organization of the voices which constitute it and the strategies by which it smoothes over the incoherences and contradictions of the ideology inscribed in it. A form of criticism which refuses to reproduce the pseudo-knowledge offered by the text provides a new knowledge of the work of literature. Such a criticism does not simply reject the classic realist text as an object of consumption, imposing a form of censorship on the mode of writing which remains dominant in our society, but works to foreground its contradictions and so to read it radically. Such a criticism finds in the literary work a different object of intelligibility: it produces the text.

THE 'COPERNICAN' REVOLUTION

Consumerist criticism has come to seem increasingly inappropriate to the new ways of understanding both language and the world developed in the twentieth century. It is probably only the continued isolation of the concept of literature itself as an autonomous and unified area of enquiry that has permitted the survival of expressive realism for so long.[1] Only by closing the doors of the English department against theoretical challenges from outside can we continue to ignore the 'Copernican' revolution which is currently taking place, and which is radically undermining traditional ways of perceiving both the world and the text.

Lacan repeatedly draws attention to Freud's comparison of his own critical reception with the reception accorded to Copernican theory in the sixteenth century. Freud, Lacan argues, decentred the human being just as Copernicus decentred the cosmos; as a result of Freud's work, 'the very centre of the human being was no longer to be found at the place assigned to it by a whole humanist tradition' (Lacan 1977a: 114).

The Copernican universe, no longer geocentric, was no longer unproblematically theocentric either. The possibility of a plurality of worlds and a plurality of atonements put in question the unique relationship between God and humanity which had been essential to Christian thinking. In conjunction with an ideological shift towards a plurality of consciences, each claiming direct access to the truth (Protestantism), and a political and economic shift towards a plurality of individual members of the bourgeoisie owing their primary allegiance to market forces, rather than to a single authority-figure (capitalism), Renaissance science initiated a process of secularization from which Christianity has never recovered. Freud, in challenging the Cartesian basis of liberal humanism, the concept of personality determined by conscious subjectivity, the transcendent mind of the unique individual, challenged the ideology of liberal humanism itself. In displacing the philosophical *cogito* ('I think, therefore I am': consciousness as the guarantee of identity), Freud by implication put in question 'the mirage that renders modern man so sure of being himself even in his uncertainties about himself, and even in the mistrust he has learned to practise against the traps of self-love' (Lacan 1977a: 165).

In practice, however, Freud's work alone has not had the resounding effect that the Copernican comparison would imply. On the contrary, Freudian psychoanalysis has been steadily recuperated by a psychoanalytic theory and practice which has the effect of upholding the existing social formation. Freudian theory has been invoked in support of sexism, biological determinism, and the bourgeois practice of analysis itself, which reintegrates the individual into society as it is. In each case it has been thought to depend on – and used to reinforce – the concept of a fixed, unchanging human nature in a world at least as fixed and unchanging as the medieval cosmos. And it is this concept of an essential human nature as the source of action and of history which has been the ally of liberal humanism against proposals for radical change.

It is therefore Lacan's reading of Freud which constitutes the basis of a genuinely Copernican revolution. Lacan consistently rejects a concept of humanity based on a quasi-biological theory of instincts, and insists that the subject is constructed in the symbolic order. The subject speaks, but only in so far as language permits the production of meaning, including the meaning of the subject's own identity, subjectivity itself. 'Man speaks, then, but it is because the symbol has made him man' (Lacan 1977a: 65). The unconscious is not a repository of biological drives but, like subjectivity, a construct, created in the moment of entry into the symbolic order, produced in the gap between the subject of the utterance, the I of the *énoncé*, and the subject of the enunciation, the I who speaks. Constructed of elements whose entry into the symbolic order is barred, the unconscious is structured like a language. Its 'speech', metaphoric and metonymic, appears in dreams, in jokes and slips of the tongue, threatening the apparent autonomy of the ego and undermining the seeming fixity of the subject-positions available in the symbolic order. Desire, the experience of lack, is the effect in the subject of the condition imposed by the division between conscious and unconscious, separated by the signifying splitting. Unfixed, unsatisfied, the human being is not a unity, not autonomous, but a process, perpetually in construction, perpetually contradictory, perpetually open to change.

Linguistic change, therefore, any alteration of the relationship between man and the signifier, 'changes the whole course of history by modifying the moorings that anchor his being' (174). And this discovery of a world without fixity, a cosmos permitting infinite movement, constitutes the Copernican revolution which Lacan attributes to Freud:

> It is precisely in this that Freudianism, however misunderstood it has been, and however confused its consequences have been, to anyone capable of perceiving the changes we have lived through in our own lives, is seen to have founded an intangible but radical revolution. There is no point in collecting witnesses to the fact: everything involving not just the human sciences, but the destiny of man, politics, metaphysics, literature, the arts, advertising, propaganda, and through these even economics, everything has been affected.
>
> (Lacan 1977a: 174)

The scientific revolution of the Renaissance was not, of course, the work of a single individual. In the same way, as Lacan suggests, the modern Copernican revolution is taking place in a number of areas simultaneously. Althusser, drawing attention to the implications of Lacan's reading of Freud, points also to the parallels with Marxism:

Since Copernicus, we have known that the earth is not the 'centre' of the universe. Since Marx, we have known that the human subject, the economic, political or philosophical ego is not the 'centre' of history – and even, in opposition to the Philosophers of the Enlightenment and to Hegel, that history has no 'centre' but possesses a structure which has no necessary 'centre' except in ideological misrecognition.

(Althusser 1971: 201)

Again there is a certain irony here. A traditional economistic Marxism had merely shifted the centre from human consciousness to the economy, much as Freudianism had shifted the centre from consciousness to the instincts. Here again the radical decentring has been the work of reinterpretation. It is Althusser's own concepts, produced in the process of reading Marx, of *structure in dominance*, *overdetermination* and *relative autonomy* which have removed the centre from history.

· The weakness of economistic Marxism was, in Althusser's view, that it retained, in its concept of the superstructure as an expression or phenomenon of the mode of production, an inverted version of Hegel's essentialism. In Marx, Althusser argues, is the material for a more complex concept of the relationship between base and superstructure: 'on the one hand, *determination in the last instance by the (economic) mode of production*; on the other, *the relative autonomy of the superstructures and their specific effectivity*' (Althusser 1969: 111). Althusser analyses the social formation in terms of three *levels* or instances of human practice, the economic, the political and the ideological. Each has its own relative autonomy, its own specific effectivity, its own contradictions. Each instance constitutes the condition of the existence of the others. Any social formation is therefore *overdetermined*, that is, produced by and producing a range of practices, and thus decentred, so that in spite of the principle of determination in the last instance by the economy, economic analysis alone is woefully inadequate. As Althusser puts it in a more than usually graphic (and much quoted) passage of *For Marx*:

the economic dialectic is never active *in the pure state*; in History, these instances, the superstructures, etc. – are never seen to step respectfully aside when their work is done or, when the Time comes, as his

> pure phenomena, to scatter before His Majesty the Economy as he
> strides along the royal road of the Dialectic. From the first moment to
> the last, the lonely hour of the 'last instance' never comes.
>
> (113)

In 'Ideology and Ideological State Apparatuses', his examination of the
relative autonomy and specific effectivity of ideological practice,
Althusser invokes the (broadly Lacanian) subject as the destination of
all ideology. In turn, it is the function of ideology to constitute concrete individuals as subjects, so that they are 'spontaneously' and
'naturally' integrated into the existing social formation, living an
imaginary relation to the real conditions of their existence, 'working by
themselves' in subjection to the constraints imposed (in the last
instance) by the mode of production.

In each of the cases I have mentioned, the decentring process
involves the dethroning of an authority – the medieval God, the transcendent *cogito*, the instincts, 'His Majesty the Economy'. In literature
the same Copernican revolution has dethroned the author, who still
reigns in consumerist criticism as the source and explanation of the
nature of the text. In practice, the author's subjectivity, itself constructed in language, is 'only a ready-formed dictionary, its words only
explainable through other words, and so on indefinitely' (Barthes
1977: 146). Unable, therefore, to 'express' a unique and transcendent
subjectivity, the author constructs a text by assembling intertextual
fragments:

> the writer can only imitate a gesture that is always anterior, never
> original. His only power is to mix writings, to counter the ones with the
> others, in such a way as never to rest on any one of them.
>
> (146)

The Death of the Author, the Absolute Subject of literature, means the
liberation of the text from the authority of a presence behind it which
gives it meaning. Released from the constraints of a single and univocal
reading, the text becomes available for production, plural, contradictory, capable of change. Like the Lacanian subject it is unfixed, a
process:

Once the Author is removed, the claim to decipher a text becomes
quite futile. To give a text an Author is to impose a limit on that text, to
furnish it with a final signified, to close the writing. . . . In the multiplicity of writing, everything is to be *disentangled*, nothing *deciphered*;
the structure can be followed, 'run' (like the thread of a stocking) at
every point and at every level, but there is nothing beneath; the space
of writing is to be ranged over, not pierced; writing ceaselessly posits
meaning ceaselessly to evaporate it, carrying out a systematic exemp-
tion of meaning. In precisely this way literature (it would be better
from now on to say *writing*), by refusing to assign a 'secret', an ultimate meaning, to the text (and to the world as text), liberates what
may be called an anti-theological activity, an activity that is truly revolutionary since to refuse to fix meaning is, in the end, to refuse God
and his hypostases – reason, science, law.

(147)

In S/Z Barthes liberates the 'parsimonious plural' of the classic realist
text, ranging over without piercing the degree of polyphony to be
found in Balzac's story. Balzac has relinquished all control: the meaning is to be produced by the reader, not consumed, ready-prepared by
the author.

But it was probably Macherey who began the work of decentring the
literary text. For Macherey it is the lack in the work, its silence, what it
is unable to say, which constitutes the evidence of its reverse side, a
contrary project threatening and undermining the conscious project:
'Freud relegated this *absence of certain words* to a new place which he was
the first to explore, and which he paradoxically *named*: the unconscious'
(Macherey 1978: 85). The unconscious of the work is constructed in
the moment of its entry into literary form, in the gap between the
project and the formulation. The process is precisely parallel to the
process by which the child enters the symbolic order. The text is a
bearer of ideological meaning, but only in so far as literary form permits the production of meaning. To adapt Lacan's formula, the text
speaks, but it is because literary form has made it a text.

What is present in the work is, finally, history – not as background,
not as cause, but as the condition of the work's existence as ideology
and as fiction:

> Thus, it is not a question of introducing a historical explanation which is stuck on to the work from the outside. On the contrary, we must show a sort of splitting within the work: this division is *its* unconscious, in so far as it possesses one – the unconscious which is history, the play of history beyond its edges, encroaching on those edges: this is why it is possible to trace the path which leads from the haunted work to that which haunts it. Once again it is not a question of redoubling the work with an unconscious, but a question of revealing in the very gestures of expression that which it is not. Then, the reverse side of what is written will be history itself.
>
> (Macherey 1978: 94)

The task of criticism, then, is to establish the unspoken in the text, to decentre it in order to produce a knowledge of history.

But if Freud decentred the individual and Marx decentred history, it was finally Saussure's decentring of language which made possible so much of the subsequent work I have mentioned. In revealing language as a system of differences with no positive terms, Saussure implicitly put in question the 'metaphysics of presence' which had dominated Western philosophy. Signs owe their capacity for signification not to the world but to their difference from each other in the network of signs which is the signifying system. Through linguistic difference 'there is born the world of meaning of a particular language in which the world of things will come to be arranged. . . . It is the world of words that creates the world of things' (Lacan 1977a: 65). What Saussure initiated, Derrida developed. In Derrida's account, meaning is no longer *seizable*, a pure intelligibility accessible to our grasp. Deferred, as well as differed, pushed out of reach, meaning becomes undecidable. Thus we can no longer understand the signifier to be preceded by an anterior truth, a meaning, the *presence* of a signified whose existence ultimately necessitates a transcendental signified (God, nature, reason) to which all truths can be referred (Derrida 1976: 49). The epoch of the metaphysics of presence is doomed, and with it all the methods of analysis, explanation and interpretation which rest on a single, unquestioned, pre-Copernican *centre*.

PRODUCING THE TEXT

In Chapter 6 I drew attention to the parallels between Macherey and Barthes without dwelling on the differences between them, but there is an important difference which should not be allowed to go unobserved. When Macherey reads Jules Verne, or when I read Conan Doyle in the light of Macherey's theory, the absences we find in the text have in one sense always been there for all to see, however differently they have been explained, or however they have been smoothed over by conventional modes of reading. If Verne's nineteenth-century readers did not identify the repressed in the text, if they did not recognize the silence with which the work finally confronts its own ideological project, it was because they read from within the same ideological framework, shared the same repressions and took for granted the same silences. If admirers of Sherlock Holmes have not recognized the implications of the elusiveness in the text (even when they have perceived the element of remaining mystery, as the conjectures about the private life of Sherlock Holmes have consistently shown), it is because they have shared so much of the ideology which constitutes the raw material of the stories. Indeed, it is still only by distancing ourselves from the familiar modes of representation that we can expect to identify the areas on which ideology is silent.

The process of literary production which is Macherey's primary concern is the production of the text by the author, the transformation of the ideological raw material by the available means of literary production. In Macherey's work the first of the elements that is new is the analysis of modes of literary production, the insistence that the text 'is not *created* by an intention (objective or subjective); it is *produced* under determinate conditions' (Macherey 1978: 78). The author as mysterious genius has disappeared, but has been replaced by a worker transforming a given raw material through the methodical employment of determinate means of production (Macherey 1978: 137; cf. Althusser 1969: 167). Criticism offers a knowledge of this mode of production and so, finally, a knowledge of history.

Criticism, too, however, in Macherey's Althusserian problematic, is a practice which *produces* knowledge, and it is in this sense that Macherey's theory is potentially more radical than his readings of specific texts might imply. The text as object of knowledge is not to be confused with the text as given, as empirical object, the text 'as it really is'. While the text as it really is will be the final object of critical knowledge, it is never given but progressively discovered:

> This means that a rigorous knowledge must beware of all forms of empiricism, for the objects of any rational investigation have no prior existence but are thought into being. The object does not pose before the interrogating eye, for thought is not the passive perception of a general disposition, as though the object should offer to share itself, like an open fruit, both displayed and concealed by a single gesture. The act of knowing is not like listening to a discourse already consti-tuted, a mere fiction which we have simply to translate. It is rather the elaboration of a new discourse, the articulation of a silence.
>
> (Macherey 1978: 5–6)

In producing a knowledge of the text, criticism actively transforms what is given. It is not a process of recognition of the truth, but work to produce meaning. No longer the accomplice of ideology, no longer parasitic on an already given literary text, criticism constructs its object, produces the work. In consequence the author loses all author-ity over the text: 'the work that the author wrote is not precisely the work that is explicated by the critic' (Macherey 1978: 7). And this is so because the distinct *practices* of writer and critic are inscribed in distinct discourses in a relationship of relative autonomy.

Barthes, in proclaiming the Death of the Author, takes the more radical of the positions implied by Macherey; when Barthes reads *Sarrasine*, or when Lacan reads Edgar Allan Poe's 'The Purloined Letter' (Lacan 1972), they concern themselves only with the second of Mach-erey's distinct practices. The processes of production performed by Balzac or by Poe are now largely irrelevant: the area of concern is a purely critical practice, the production of meaning by the work of *reading* the text, in which the text constitutes the raw material to be transformed by the critic.

But how is this work of transformation accomplished? What, to use the Althusserian model again, corresponds in critical practice to the means of production? The question is important because there is a

danger that this new critical practice could tumble back into subjec-
tivism, into an individualistic quest for increasing ingenuities of
meaning-production, or into relativism, the conviction that the text
means whatever it 'obviously' means within a given social formation,
and no more. In practice, when Barthes reads *Sarrasine*, he transforms it
by the application of existing forms of knowledge, employing post-
Saussurean linguistics, Lacanian psychoanalysis and Marxist economic
theory to produce a meaning which was literally not available to Balzac
and his contemporary readers. Without wanting to deny, therefore, the
enormous ingenuity of S/Z, we cannot retreat into a position which
attributes Barthes's reading of *Sarrasine* to the individual brilliance of its
author. This would be merely to reconstitute Barthes himself as the
'genius' of ideological critical theory in its pre-Copernican phase. On
the contrary, *Sarrasine* can be produced in our time, which is in a sense
to say written rather than read, by employing the knowledge pertinent
to our time rather than the nineteenth century.[2]

Possibilities of meaning are not discovered by transcendent geniuses
who cleverly (and perversely) refuse the obvious reading: on the contrary, they circulate between text, ideology and readers whose subjectivity is discursively constructed and so displaced across a range of
knowledges. Thus author and reader (even when these are conceived as
ideal types created by the formal strategies of the text) no longer present the symmetrical poles of an intersubjective process understood as
communication. Instead, critical practice is seen as a process of releas-
ing the positions from which the text is intelligible. Liberated from the
fixity of the communication model, the text is available for production
in the process of reading.

What a Machereyan reading supplies is a knowledge of history,
albeit the unconscious of history, while the readings of Barthes and
Lacan are unequivocally of the present and for the present. In one sense
the difference is a matter of degree: history is perceived by and from
the present, produced with the analytical tools of the present, and
explanatory in relation to the present. But in another sense the difference is one of kind: the process of transformation which acknowledges
no obligation to history appropriates the text for the present in a more
fundamental way. As an instance of the way in which it is possible to
transform the raw material of the text, it is illuminating to consider

Lacan's 'Seminar on "The Purloined Letter"'. (It is also important to point out, however, that this extremely dense, complex and perpetually surprising critical text is not readily summarized. The 'Seminar' assumes a working knowledge of Freudian theory as well as of Lacan's readings of Freud and Saussure. The reader will perhaps bear with me if I fail either to do it justice on the one hand, or to render it absolutely lucid on the other.)

Edgar Allan Poe's story, 'The Purloined Letter', is an early and apparently relatively straightforward detective story. It concerns a letter addressed to a woman of high rank, who is almost certainly the Queen. The letter, whose existence must at all costs be concealed from her husband, is stolen in the presence of the King, and replaced by a substitute letter, while the Queen watches, by a Minister, whose possession of the letter gives him an unspecified power. The Queen asks the police to recover the letter. They search the Minister's hotel with the most detailed attention, but without success, and finally the Prefect of Police is compelled to ask for the help of Dupin, Poe's detective. Dupin succeeds in locating the letter, which is not concealed, as the police had mistakenly assumed, but is on display in a card-rack, disguised and slightly crumpled. Dupin diverts the attention of the Minister and takes the opportunity of replacing the letter with a substitute letter of his own, which expresses his rage against the Minister for his action.

Lacan reads Poe's story as a parable – a fable, as he calls it – of psychoanalytic theory, and at the same time as a source of knowledge about the workings of the process of signification. Since the Poe tale clearly bears some resemblance to the Sherlock Holmes stories I have discussed, and in particular to 'The Second Stain', Lacan's very radical reading of it offers a useful demonstration of the extent to which the original text is transformed (produced) by his work.

Lacan's reading turns on the double meaning of 'letter' – as epistle, but also as typographical character, the letter which, though it is itself without meaning, constitutes the unit of difference in language, the phoneme which, by differentiating, makes meaning possible. When Lacan describes the letter to the Queen as 'the symbol of a pact', the existence of which 'situates her in a symbolic chain foreign to the one which constitutes her faith' (Lacan 1972: 58), the vocabulary evokes his own theory of the unconscious, structured like a language, which is divided from the conscious self that is constructed in, and identifies with, the system of differences constituted by the symbolic order. The displaced letter is evidence of the division in the self between consciousness and the unconscious, site of another set of signifiers. It is the repeated insistence of the (displaced) unconscious signifiers which constitutes the return of the repressed in dreams and slips of the tongue. Their meaning cannot be consciously acknowledged, just as the Queen's 'possession of the letter is impossible to bring forward publicly as legitimate'. At a primary level of Lacan's reading Dupin is the analyst who identifies the displaced signifier and restores it to its place but, himself caught up in the analytic process, becomes trapped in the circuits of transference and counter-transference.

The tale reveals the nature of the construction of the subject in the symbolic order. In an etymological excursion Lacan discovers that to purloin is to put aside; thus 'we are quite simply dealing with a letter which has been diverted from its path' (59), which has left its place, even though it returns to it by a circuitous route. And thus, for Lacan, the story is an allegory of the relationship between the self and signification:

> If what Freud discovered and rediscovers with a perpetually increasing sense of shock has a meaning, it is that the displacement of the signifier determines the subjects in their acts, in their destiny, in their refusals, in their blindnesses, in their end and in their fate, their innate gifts and social acquisitions notwithstanding, without regard for character or sex, and that, willingly or not, everything that might be considered the stuff of psychology, kit and caboodle, will follow the path of the signifier.
>
> (60)

Each holder of the stolen letter in turn necessarily repeats the symbolic situation, which shows how the signifying chain both binds and blinds. Action against the author of the letter is not in question: to whom, after all, does language belong? The story reveals 'that sign of contradiction and scandal constituted by the letter', source of the divided, contradictory subject. The power the Minister derives from possessing the letter, an ascendancy over the Queen, is betrayed by the role the letter constructs for him: he becomes increasingly transformed in the image of the Queen, to the point where he surrenders the letter to Dupin just as the Queen has earlier permitted him to steal it.

But this is not all. In Lacan's reading, the tale also supplies a knowledge of the nature of fiction. In a dizzying sequence of statements he argues that fiction, precisely because it appears to create its own laws, demonstrates most fully the rules of the symbolic order, which in practice are the conditions of its possibility, as they are the conditions of the possibility of subjectivity. The story, which presents itself as fiction, offers to a reader able to analyse it, a *knowledge*, albeit displaced, of the laws of both its own and the reader's (contradictory) construction:

> Which is why we have decided to illustrate for you today the truth which may be drawn from that moment in Freud's thought under study – namely, that it is the symbolic order which is constitutive for the subject – by demonstrating in a story the decisive orientation which the subject receives from the itinerary of a signifier.
>
> It is that truth, let us note, which makes the very existence of fiction possible. And in that case, a fable is as appropriate as any other narrative for bringing it to light – at the risk of having the fable's coherence put to the test in the process. Aside from that reservation, a fictive tale even has the advantage of manifesting symbolic necessity more purely to the extent that we may believe its conception arbitrary.

(40)

THE PROBLEMS

Is literature most usefully seen as a means of access to history (Macherey), or as a way of grasping the present (Lacan and Barthes)? Perhaps the distinction is false? There is no way of grasping the present without a knowledge of history, of the present as part of the process of history. But to understand the text in its historical specificity is not the same as to set it free from its historical moorings, reading it as the work of the present.

Shakespeare the Elizabethan, or Shakespeare our Contemporary? In a way we have no choice. The text from the past roots itself in history through its unfamiliar allusions, its archaic references, the conventions of its period. Paradoxically, however, these features have the effect of reminding us that we are not Elizabethans, cannot experience the text as they experienced it, but can only use the text as a basis for the reconstruction of an ideology which is the source of its silences.

As I have argued, meanings circulate between text, ideology and reader, and the work of criticism is to release possible meanings. The reading practices of Macherey and Lacan are not in competition, and it is only within the old framework which invests the text with a single authoritative meaning that they seem to be so. An adequate critical practice includes both modes of reading, but it recognizes the difference between them and knows which it practises in a particular instance.

But a more radical problem arises in terms of the question whether we should continue to speak of literature at all. If we accept the case for the primacy of the signifier, it becomes clear that the existence of the term gives no particular authority to the assumption that there is a body of texts, with their own specific practices, which can usefully be isolated as 'literature'. Quite apart from the value-judgments frequently but not invariably implicit in the term (George Eliot is literature, Barbara Cartland is probably not, but literature on double-glazing might be pushed through the letter box), it is not at all apparent that it is helpful to isolate other forms, whether written or not – advertising, for instance, or film – from the form we call literary. I have used the word here, but reluctantly, 'under erasure', as Derrida puts it when of necessity he employs terms belonging to a theoretical and discursive framework which is undermined by his work as a whole.

I hope at least to have suggested that criticism can no longer be isolated from other areas of knowledge. The new critical practice requires us to come to terms with concepts of ideology and subjectivity drawn from fields which have no relation to a theory or practice of literary criticism conceived as self-contained. Traditional boundaries, constructed in language and in ideology, no longer hold, even though it is not immediately clear how to contemplate the alarming prospect of a world in which there are no final and uncontested divisions because there are no ultimate determinable meanings, no transcendental signified.

And it is here, perhaps, that we encounter in its most striking form one of the problems of the new Copernican cosmos. Derrida's universe, for example, where there is only the infinite play of difference, is, as he recognizes, literally unthinkable. Barthes, refusing 'reason, science, law', fearing the tyranny of lucidity, leaves as his only unequivocal positive the concept of a 'writable' text, infinitely plural, infinitely open to production, but by definition unable to exist. And there is an alternative danger – of refusing to surrender the last vestiges of the centre. Althusser's ideology, relatively autonomous, with its own effectivity, functions, none the less, on behalf of the mode of production, a position which leaves the concept of relative autonomy very uncertain. And in some of Lacan's formulations it seems as if the unconscious is offered as essential, the true nucleus of our being in a way that conciousness is not, and there is a danger here of inverting the Cartesian problematic rather than doing away with it.

These concepts, in other words, are still vulnerable, still in many ways precarious. But this means only that there is more work to be done. Copernicus merely began a rethinking of cosmology which Galileo, Newton and Einstein continued, and the work still remains incomplete. The fact that the new critical practice does not constitute a closed and watertight system is the source and evidence of its vitality. The questions which remain within it are not a reason for retreat. Rather they invite us to go on to solve the problems which new forms of understanding must inevitably generate, to produce a critical practice which is fully pertinent to those forms of understanding, without evading the difficulties necessarily involved in the development of a new mode of production.

Further Reading

The field of theory is now so large, and people's familiarity with it so varied, that suggestions for further reading can do no more than indicate lines of enquiry. I have made one assumption, however: that the best way to find out about theory is to read more theory. I begin with the most accessible works, before going on to list more difficult material under five specific headings.

ACCESSIBLE

Antony Easthope and Kate McGowan have assembled some of what are now the classic texts in *A Critical and Cultural Theory Reader* (Buckingham: Open University Press, 1992).

Roland Barthes, *Mythologies* (London: Vintage, 1993) and *The Eiffel Tower and Other Mythologies* (Berkeley: University of California Press, 1997) offer witty, inventive instances of some of the earliest work in semiology. Barthes's *A Lover's Discourse: Fragments* (Harmondsworth: Penguin, 1990) is a delight.

Marjorie Garber, *Vested Interests: Cross-Dressing and Cultural Anxiety* (Harmondsworth: Penguin, 1993) wears its semiological and psychoanalytic sophistication lightly in an account of some transgressions of conventional gender categories.

Edward Said's *Orientalism* (Harmondsworth: Penguin, 1995) brought Michel Foucault's work to bear on colonialism. Since the first edition of *Orientalism* in 1985, Homi Bhabha, *The Location of Culture* (London: Routledge, 1994) has touched a nerve, as has Robert Young, *Colonial Desire: Hybridity in Theory, Culture and Race* (New York: Routledge, 1995). Julia Kristeva has explored some of the implications of immigration in a characteristic mixture of theory and confession in *Strangers to Ourselves* (New York: Columbia University Press, 1991).

For Foucault himself, see *Discipline and Punish* (Harmondsworth: Penguin, 1979). His *History of Sexuality: An Introduction* (Harmondsworth: Penguin, 1990) constitutes an inaugural text for queer studies.

Raymond Williams saw the implications of the inscription of value in language in *Keywords: A Vocabulary of Culture and Society* (London: Fontana, 1976).

Slavoj Žižek is always good value, especially on films. Try *The Sublime Object of Ideology* (London: Verso, 1989) and *Looking Awry* (Cambridge, MA: MIT Press, 1991).

I have put some of the theory to work in *Desire: Love Stories in Western Culture* (Oxford: Blackwell, 1994) and *Shakespeare and the Loss of Eden* (Basingstoke: Macmillan, 1999).

Antony Easthope in *Privileging Difference* (Basingstoke: Palgrave, 2002) takes a number of theorists to task in a good-humoured way for betraying the most radical insights of post-Saussurean theory.

LANGUAGE

Emile Benveniste, *Problems in General Linguistics* (Miami: University of Miami Press, 1971). See especially 'Subjectivity in Language', pp. 223–30.

Ferdinand de Saussure, *Course in General Linguistics*, tr. Wade Baskin (London: Fontana, 1974). See especially the chapter on 'Linguistic Value', pp. 111–22. NB the later Roy Harris translation does not use the conventional vocabulary of signifier and signified, and so obscures the influence of Saussure on what came later.

V. N. Vološinov, *Marxism and the Philosophy of Language*, tr. Ladislav Matejka and I. R. Titunik (New York: Seminar Press, 1973). This is remarkable as one of the earliest recognitions of the importance of Saussure's *Course*. It was begun in Lenin's post-revolutionary Russia, but Stalin would soon clamp down on such radical work.

IDEOLOGY

The classic texts are Karl Marx and Friedrich Engels, *The German Ideology*, Part 1 (there are any number of editions of this) and Louis Althusser, 'Ideology and Ideological State Apparatuses', *Lenin and Philosophy and Other Essays*, tr. Ben Brewster (London: New Left Books, 1971), pp. 121–73.

Other important essays by Althusser include 'Contradiction and Over-determination' and 'Marxism and Humanism' in his *For Marx*, tr. Ben Brewster (Harmondsworth: Penguin, 1969), pp. 87–128, 219–47.

Barry Hindess and Paul Hirst are (sympathetically) critical of Althusser in *Mode of Production and Social Formation* (London: Macmillan, 1977). See also Paul Hirst, *On Law and Ideology* (London: Macmillan, 1979), which includes Hirst 1976.

LITERATURE, CULTURE

Very little current cultural analysis remains untouched by post-Saussurean theory, and much literary criticism now takes account of it in one way or another. For an instance, see Nicholas Royle ed., *Deconstructions: A User's Guide* (Basingstoke: Palgrave, 2000).

Linda Hutcheon is always highly readable. See, for example, *A Poetics of Postmodernism: History, Theory, Fiction* (London: Routledge, 1992).

Shoshana Felman is at home with deconstruction and psychoanalysis: *What Does a Woman Want? Reading and Sexual Difference* (Baltimore, MD: Johns Hopkins University Press, 1993).

Barbara Johnson is also a highly sophisticated reader: *A World of Difference* (Baltimore, MD: Johns Hopkins University Press, 1987).

The classic works are by Roland Barthes: *S/Z*, tr. Richard Miller (Oxford: Blackwell, 1990) and *The Pleasure of the Text*, tr. Richard Miller (London: Cape, 1976).

Barthes's 'The Death of the Author' is available in *Modern Criticism and Theory: A Reader*, ed. David Lodge (London: Longman, 1988), pp. 167–72, as is Michel Foucault, 'What is an Author?', pp. 197–210.

Pierre Macherey's *A Theory of Literary Production*, tr. Geoffrey Wall (London: Routledge and Kegan Paul, 1978) remains unsurpassed. It may have been too complex ever to have elicited the full attention it deserves.

Among the antecedents of Barthes and Macherey, Bertolt Brecht was an influential figure: *Brecht on Theatre*, ed. and tr. John Willett (London: Eyre Methuen, 1964). See especially pp. 33–42, 69–77 and 179–205.

Some of Stephen Heath's classic essays from *Screen* are reprinted in his *Questions of Cinema* (London: Macmillan, 1981).

PSYCHOANALYSIS

Nothing Lacan wrote was easy. However, the seminars are slightly more approachable than his writings. *Seminar 7* includes a reading of *Antigone*: Jacques Lacan, *The Ethics of Psychoanalysis, 1959–60*, tr. Dennis Potter (London: Routledge, 1992), pp. 241–87. Lacan's exposition of the gaze in *Seminar 11* has been influential in art history and film theory: *The Four Fundamental Concepts of Psychoanalysis*, tr. Alan Sheridan (Harmondsworth: Penguin, 1994), pp. 65–119. But for the essay on 'The Mirror Stage', as well as 'The Significa-tion of the Phallus' you need the *Ecrits*, tr. Alan Sheridan (London: Tavistock, 1977), pp. 1–7, pp. 281–91.

Help is available from Malcolm Bowie, *Lacan* (London: Fontana, 1991) and Jane Gallop, *Reading Lacan* (Ithaca, NY: Cornell University Press, 1985). You can trust Dylan Evans, *An Introductory Dictionary of Lacanian Psychoanalysis* (London: Routledge, 1996).

It also helps to be familiar with Freud. The case histories are very readable – and illuminating at the same time: Sigmund Freud and Josef Breuer, *Studies on Hysteria*, The Penguin Freud Library 3 (Harmondsworth: Penguin, 1974); Sigmund Freud, *Case Histories 1, 'Dora' and 'Little Hans'*, The Penguin Freud Library 8 (Harmondsworth: Penguin, 1977). *The Interpretation of Dreams* is still the big one in every sense: The Penguin Freud Library 4 (Harmondsworth: Penguin, 1976).

Slavoj Žižek appropriates psychoanalysis to construct a social theory of antagonism. He is not as Lacanian, in my view, as he claims, but is no less interesting for that: *Enjoy Your Symptom! Jacques Lacan in Hollywood and Out* (New York: Routledge, 2000).

DECONSTRUCTION

There is no easy way to learn to read Derrida, either. He is often at his most intelligible in interviews, which the French take more seriously than we do. I have learnt a lot from Jacques Derrida, *Positions* (London: Althlone, 1987).

His *Monolingualism of the Other; or, The Prosthesis of Origin* (Stanford, CA: Stanford University Press, 1998) is decidedly approachable and queries the logic of nationalism, totalitarianism, etc.

Among other later works, *Aporias* (Stanford CA: Stanford University Press, 1993) is about death; *Specters of Marx* (New York: Routledge, 1994) argues that we cannot afford to forget Marxism (and analyses the opening scenes of *Hamlet*); and *The Gift of Death* (Chicago: University of Chicago Press, 1995) is about ethics (not death).

The Postcard: From Socrates to Freud and Beyond (Chicago: University of Chicago Press, 1987) is playful, elusive, fascinating. The first half is a (sort of) love story; the second deconstructs Freud and Lacan (the latter with uncharacteristic vehemence).

Ultimately, however, *Of Grammatology*, tr. Gayatri Chakravorty Spivak (Baltimore, MD: Johns Hopkins University Press, 1997) is inescapable. For Derrida's deconstruction of Saussure, see pp. 27–73.

NOTES

1 They were anticipated in this by T. S. Eliot, who derived from T. E. Hulme a belief that the poetic experience exists only in the specific formulation of it. This element in Eliot's theory is directly contradicted, of course, by his more influential expressive concept of the 'objective correlative' (Krieger 1997: 51–6)

2 For further discussion of this point, see Hawkes 1977: 151–6; Fekete 1977: 85–103.

3 For a subsequent apology for New Criticism, however, see Wellek 1978.

4 The problem of prepositions and conjunctions, which presents something of an obstacle to the empiricist theory of language, is summarily despatched: 'only large and striking symbols are likely to be treated critically as signs: nouns and verbs, and phrases built up out of important words. Prepositions and conjunctions are almost pure connectives. A dictionary, which is primarily a table of conventional sign-values, can tell us nothing about such words unless we already understand them' (Frye 1957: 79).

5 For a discussion of the some of the ideological implications of Frye's work, see Fekete 1977: 107–31.

NOTE TO CHAPTER 3

1 See Barthes 1975: 17. Note, however, that *signifié* is here consistently mistranslated as 'signifier'.

NOTES TO CHAPTER 4

1 For an excellent exposition of Althusser's theory of ideology, see Hirst 1979: 22–39. But for a critique of its functionalism, see Hirst 1976. Hirst here argues that Althusser's position is problematic: it proposes both that ideology is relatively autonomous, with its own specific practices and effectivity (an important break with the classical Marxist conception of ideology as an effect of the economic base), and at the same time that ideology *functions on behalf of* the capitalist mode of production. This paper also raises other important problems, some of which can be at least partly resolved by reference to the theory of the role of language in the construction of subjectivity.
2 Hirst criticizes the concept of 'representation' here on the grounds that the term implies that the 'represented' exists outside the process of its presentation (Hirst 1976: 407–11). This objection ignores Althusser's debt to Saussure: what is presented or, in ordinary language, represented, is the effect of the signifier. I have retained the ordinary term on the grounds that it emphasizes one of the important characteristics of ideology, namely its familiarity. Ideology is always repeated, always re-presented, always already known from other usages, images and myths. Ideology re-presents not the real, nor a distorted reflection of the real, but the obvious. What it suppresses is its own construction in signifying practice.
3 The signals emitted by bees preclude the possibility of dialogue and are therefore not to be confused with language (Benveniste 1971: 49–54; Lacan 1977a: 84–5).
4 I do not exclude classic realist drama from consideration, but here irony is easiest of all to establish, since it appears in the discrepancy between what the characters believe and what is shown on the stage. In film the camera performs the role of the 'invisible' author.

NOTES TO CHAPTER 5

1 To this extent it has much in common with the 'polyphonic novel' which the Russian formalist, Mikhail Bakhtin, attributes to Dostoevsky. Bakhtin establishes a contrast between the 'monologic' or homophonic

novel, which contains all its voices within a single authorial world-view, and the 'dialogic' or polyphonic text, which embraces a multiplicity of equal voices. He says of Dostoevsky:

> It is not a multitude of characters and fates within a unified, object-ive world, illuminated by the author's unified consciousness that unfolds in his works, but precisely the *plurality of equal conscious-nesses and their worlds*, which are combined here in the unity of a given event, while at the same time retaining their unmergedness.
>
> (Bakhtin 1973: 4)

The result is a 'fundamental unfinalizedness and dialogic openness' (229). But true to the formalist principles Bakhtin adheres to in this work, he insists that he is concerned only with the aesthetic implica-tions of polyphony, and not with meaning. Since he is interested in the author's position, rather than the reader's, he does not pursue the question of the effect of the form he identifies, but it is one of the contradictions of formalism that it is hard to say anything very interest-ing about form without revealing certain assumptions about meaning. Bakhtin, whose observations are very interesting indeed, seems to work on the basis that the main consequences of polyphony are a profound respect for and analysis of 'the man in man', subjectivity, point of view. The subject in question, however, is seen as a process or, as Bakhtin puts it, consciousness is essentially 'unfinalizable' (55–6).

2   Tragi-comedy in the sense that, though the events of Acts I–III resemble the events of tragedy, the treatment of them is in a much lower key than in Shakespeare's tragedies in general, and the text often verges on comedy (e.g. II. ii. 27–129).

NOTES TO CHAPTER 6

1   In some of Macherey's formulations it is possible to identify a survival of the idealist concept of ideology as a system of free-floating ideas, 'expressed' in a work of literature (Macherey 1978: 132, 262). In response, however, to a question about how his work had changed since the publication of *A Theory of Literary Production* in 1966, Macherey alluded to Althusser's ISAs essay, stressing its importance in permitting a break with the 'unsatisfactory' conception of ideology as 'ideas in people's heads' (Macherey 1977: 5). There is no serious difficulty in reconciling Macherey's earlier position with Althusser's:

literature, as a ideological practice, retains its own specificity, its own forms of signification, and it is in bringing these into conjunction with other discursive forms that literature is able to present an implicit critique of ideology.

2 Macherey has been criticized for treating as his main example fiction peripheral to the canon (Jules Verne), and in discussing Sherlock Holmes I am perhaps perpetuating the impression that Macherey's mode of analysis cannot work with canonical literature. But for a Machereyan analysis of a series of thoroughly canonical texts, see Eagleton 1976.

NOTE TO CHAPTER 7

1 This account of Irish history is assembled from a range of sources: Boyce 1996; Brown 1999; Fitzpatrick 1977; Foster 1988; and Greaves 1991. I am grateful for help and advice on this from Claire Connolly.

NOTES TO CHAPTER 8

1 For an attack on the autonomy of literature, see Bennett 1979.

2 In a similar way, when Althusser reads Marx and Lacan reads Freud, they release the possible systematic meanings from texts which are themselves contradictory. The contradictions have been suppressed by traditional Marxism and psychoanalysis, which has sought to extract in each case a single, coherent and univocal reading, *authorized* by Marx or Freud. Althusser's Marxism makes no pretence of being 'what Marx thought', but offers itself as the product of Marx's work, a product which there is no guarantee that Marx himself would have acknowledged.

REFERENCES

Althusser, Louis, 1969. *For Marx*, tr. Ben Brewster (Harmondsworth: Penguin Books).

—— 1971. *Lenin and Philosophy and Other Essays*, tr. Ben Brewster (London: New Left Books).

Arnold, Matthew, 1965. *Poems*, ed. Kenneth Allot (London: Longman).

Bakhtin, Mikhail, 1973. *Problems of Dostoevsky's Poetics*, tr. R. W. Rotsel (Michigan: Ardis/Ann Arbor).

Barthes, Roland, 1975. *S/Z*, tr. Richard Miller (London: Cape).

—— 1977. *Image-Music-Text*, tr. Stephen Heath (London: Fontana).

—— 1993. *Mythologies*, tr. Annette Lavers (London: Vintage).

Bennett, Tony, 1979. *Formalism and Marxism* (London: Methuen).

Benoist, Jean-Marie, 1971. 'La Géométrie des Poètes Métaphysiques', *Critique* 27, 730–69.

Benveniste, Emile, 1971. *Problems in General Linguistics* (Miami: University of Miami Press).

Berger, John and Mohr, Jean, 1976. *A Fortunate Man* (London: Writers and Readers Publishing Cooperative).

Booth, Wayne C., 1961. *The Rhetoric of Fiction* (Chicago: University of Chicago Press).

Boyce, D. George, 1996. '1916, Interpreting the Rising', *The Making of Modern Irish History: Revisionism and the Revisionist Controversy*, ed. D. George Boyce and Alan O'Day (London: Routledge).

Brecht, Bertolt, 1964. *Brecht on Theatre*, ed. and tr. John Willett (London: Eyre Methuen).

Brontë, Charlotte, 1966. *Jane Eyre*, ed. Q. D. Leavis (Harmondsworth: Penguin Books).

Brooks, Cleanth, 1968. *The Well-Wrought Urn, Studies in the Structure of Poetry* (London: Dennis Dobson).

Brown, Terence, 1999. *The Life of W. B. Yeats: A Critical Biography* (Oxford: Blackwell).

Caputo, John D., ed., 1997. *Deconstruction in a Nutshell* (New York: Fordham University Press).

Conrad, Joseph, 1973. *Heart of Darkness* (Harmondsworth: Penguin Books).

Coward, Rosalind and Ellis, John, 1977. *Language and Materialism* (London: Routledge and Kegan Paul).

Culler, Jonathan, 1976. *Saussure* (London: Fontana).

Derrida, Jacques, 1973. 'Differance', *Speech and Phenomena and other Essays on Husserl's Theory of Signs*, tr. David B. Allison (Evanston, IL: Northwestern University Press), 129–60.

—— 1993. *Aporias*, tr. Thomas Dutoit (Stanford, CA: Stanford University Press).

—— 1994. *Specters of Marx: The State of the Debt, the Work of Mourning and the New International*, tr. Peggy Kamuf (New York: Routledge).

—— 1997a. *Of Grammatology*, tr. Gayatri Chakravorty Spivak (Baltimore and London: Johns Hopkins University Press).

—— 1997b. *Politics of Friendship*, tr. George Collins (London: Verso).

De Waal, Ronald, 1972. *The World Bibliography of Sherlock Holmes* (Greenwich, CT.: New York Graphic Society).

Dickens, Charles, 1966. *Oliver Twist*, ed. P. Fairclough (Harmondsworth: Penguin Books).

Donne, John, 1971. *The Complete English Poems*, ed. A. J. Smith (Harmondsworth: Penguin Books).

Doyle, Arthur Conan, 1950. *The Memoirs of Sherlock Holmes* (Harmondsworth: Penguin Books).

—— 1976. *The Return of Sherlock Holmes* (London: Pan Books).

Eagleton, Terry, 1975. *Myths of Power, a Marxist Study of the Brontës* (London: Macmillan).

—— 1976. *Criticism and Ideology* (London: New Left Books).

—— 1977. 'Ecriture and Eighteenth-Century Fiction', *Literature, Society and the Sociology of Literature*, Proceedings of the Conference held at the University of Essex, July, 1976 (University of Essex).

Eliot, George, 1965. *Middlemarch*, ed. W. J. Harvey (Harmondsworth: Penguin Books).

—— 1976. *The Mill on the Floss* (London: Dent).

Fekete, John, 1977. *The Critical Twilight* (London: Routledge and Kegan Paul).

Fish, Stanley E., 1972. *Self-Consuming Artifacts: The Experience of Seventeenth-Century Literature* (Berkeley: University of California Press).

—— 1980. *Is There a Text in This Class? The Authority of Interpretive Communities* (Cambridge, MA: Harvard University Press).

—— 1989. *Doing What Comes Naturally: Change, Rhetoric, and the Practice of Theory in Literary and Legal Studies* (Oxford: Clarendon Press).

Fitzpatrick, David. 1977. *Politics and Irish Life 1913–21: Provincial Experience of War and Revolution* (Dublin: Gill and Macmillan).

Foster, R. F., 1988. *Modern Ireland 1600–1972* (London: Allen Lane).

Frye, Northrop, 1957. *Anatomy of Criticism* (Princeton: Princeton University Press).

—— 1972. 'Literature as Context: Milton's *Lycidas*', *Twentieth-Century Literary Criticism, A Reader*, ed. David Lodge (London: Longman).

Greaves, C. Desmond, 1991. *1916 As History: The Myth of the Blood Sacrifice* (Dublin: The Fulcrum Press).

Hardwick, Michael and Hardwick, Mollie, 1962. *The Sherlock Holmes Companion* (London: John Murray).

Hardy, Barbara, 1964. *The Appropriate Form, an Essay on the Novel* (London: Athlone Press).

Hawkes, Terence, 1977. *Structuralism and Semiotics* (London: Methuen).

Heath, Stephen, 1974. 'Lessons from Brecht', *Screen* vol. 15, no. 2, 103–28.

—— 1975. 'Film and System, Terms of Analysis', Part I, *Screen*, vol. 16, no. 1, 7–77; Part II, *Screen*, vol. 16, no. 2, 91–113.

1976. 'Narrative Space', *Screen*, vol. 17, no. 3, 68–112.

1976–77. 'Anata Mo', *Screen*, vol. 17, no. 4, 49–66.

1977–78. 'Notes on Suture', *Screen*, vol. 18, no. 4, 48–76.

Heinemann, Margot, 1977. 'Shakespearean Contradictions and Social Change', *Science and Society* 41, 7–16.

Hindess, Barry and Hirst, Paul, 1977. *Mode of Production and Social Formation* (London: Macmillan).

Hirst, Paul, 1976. 'Althusser's Theory of Ideology', *Economy and Society* 5, 385–412.

—— 1979. *On Law and Ideology* (London: Macmillan).

Hjelmslev, Louis, 1969. *Prolegomena to a Theory of Language*, tr. Francis J. Whitfield (Madison, Wis.: University of Wisconsin Press).

Iser, Wolfgang, 1978. *The Act of Reading* (London: Routledge and Kegan Paul).

James, Henry, 1908. *What Maisie Knew* (New York: Scribner).

Jauss, Hans Robert, 1974. 'Literary History as a Challenge to Literary Theory', *New Directions in Literary History*, ed. Ralph Cohen (London: Routledge and Kegan Paul), 11–41.

Krieger, Murray, 1977. *The New Apologists for Poetry* (Westport, CT.: Greenwood Press).

Lacan, Jacques, 1972. 'Seminar on "The Purloined Letter" ', tr. J. Mehlman, *Yale French Studies* 48, 38–72.

—— 1977a. *Ecrits*, tr. Alan Sheridan (London: Tavistock).

—— 1977b. *The Four Fundamental Concepts of Psychoanalysis*, tr. Alan Sheridan (London: Hogarth Press).

Langbaum, Robert, 1963. *The Poetry of Experience* (New York: Norton).

Leavis, F. R., 1962. *The Great Tradition* (Harmondsworth: Penguin Books).

—— 1973. *D. H. Lawrence: Novelist* (Harmondsworth: Penguin Books).

—— 1976. *The Common Pursuit* (Harmondsworth: Penguin Books).

Lemaire, Anika, 1977. *Jacques Lacan*, tr. David Macey (London: Routledge and Kegan Paul).

Lodge, David, 1978. *Changing Places* (Harmondsworth: Penguin Books).

Lukács, Georg, 1950. *Studies in European Realism*, tr. E. Bone (London: Merlin Press).

MacCabe, Colin, 1974. 'Realism and the Cinema: Notes on Some Brechtian Theses', *Screen*, vol. 15, no. 2, 7–27.

—— 1976. 'Theory and Film: Principles of Realism and Pleasure', *Screen*, vol. 17, no. 3, 7–27.

Macherey, Pierre, 1977. 'An Interview with Pierre Macherey', ed.and tr. Colin Mercer and Jean Radford, *Red Letters* 5, 3–9.

—— 1978. *A Theory of Literary Production*, tr. Geoffrey Wall (London: Routledge and Kegan Paul).

Marlowe, Christopher, 1973. *The Complete Works*, ed. Fredson Bowers (Cambridge: Cambridge University Press).

Marvell, Andrew, 1972. *The Complete Poems*, ed. Elizabeth Story Donno (Harmondsworth: Penguin Books).

Miller, Jacques-Alain, 1977–78. 'Suture (Elements of the Logic of the Signifier)', *Screen*, vol. 18, no. 4, 24–34.

Murdoch, Iris, 1977. *The Fire and the Sun: Why Plato Banished the Artists* (Oxford: Clarendon Press).

Neale, Steve, 1977. 'Propaganda', *Screen*, vol. 18, no. 3, 9–40.

Newton-De Molina, David, 1976. *On Literary Intention* (Edinburgh: Edinburgh University Press).

Nowell-Smith, Geoffrey, 1976. 'A Note on History/Discourse', *Edinburgh 76 Magazine* 1, 26–32.

Ruskin, John, 1903–12. *Works* (39 vols, London: George Allen).

Saussure, Ferdinand de, 1974. *Course in General Linguistics*, tr. Wade Baskin (London: Fontana).

Shakespeare, William, 1951. *The Complete Works*, ed. Peter Alexander (London: Collins).

Slatoff, Walter J., 1970. *With Respect to Readers: Dimensions of Literary Response* (Ithaca: Cornell University Press).

Todorov, Tzvetan, 1966. 'Les Catégories du Récit Littéraire', *Communications* 8, 125–47.

—— 1970. 'Language and Literature', *The Structuralist Controversy*, eds Richard Macksey and Eugenio Donato (Baltimore, MD: Johns Hopkins University Press), 125–33.

Wellek, René, 1963. *Concepts of Criticism* (New Haven, CT: Yale University Press).

—— 1978. 'The New Criticism: Pro and Contra', *Critical Inquiry* 4, 611–24.

Wilkenfeld, Roger B., 1969. 'The Argument of "The Scholar-Gipsy"', *Victorian Poetry* 7, 117–28.

Willemen, Paul, 1978. 'Notes on Subjectivity – on Reading "Subjectivity under Siege"', *Screen* vol. 19, no. 1, 41–69.

Williamson, Judith, 1978. *Decoding Advertisements* (London: Marion Boyars).

Wimsatt, W. K. Jr., 1970. *The Verbal Icon: Studies in the Meaning of Poetry* (London: Methuen).

Wood, D. C., 1979. 'An Introduction to Derrida', *Radical Philosophy* 21, 18–28.

Wordsworth, William, 1959. *The Prelude*, ed. E. de Selincourt, revised by Helen Darbishire (Oxford: OUP).

—— 1974. *Prose Works*, eds W. J. B. Owen and Jane Worthington Smyser (Oxford: OUP).

—— 1977. *Poems*, ed. J. O. Hayden (Harmondsworth: Penguin Books).

Yeats, W. B., 1958. *Collected Poems* (London: Macmillan).

INDEX